D0667554

# EBBY
## HALLIDAY

THE FIRST LADY
OF REAL ESTATE

# EBBY
# HALLIDAY

MICHAEL POSS

Brown Books Publishing Group
Dallas, Texas

# Ebby Halliday:
# The First Lady of Real Estate

© 2009 Michael Poss

Manufactured in the United States of America.

For information, please contact:

Brown Books Publishing Group

16200 North Dallas Parkway, Suite 170

Dallas, Texas 75248

www.brownbooks.com

972-381-0009

A New Era in Publishing™

ISBN-13: 978-1-934812-32-7

ISBN-10: 1-934812-32-3

LCCN: 2008939475

1 2 3 4 5 6 7 8 9 10

# CONTENTS

# Acknowledgments

This book would not have been possible without the tenacity of Mary Frances Burleson, president and CEO of Ebby Halliday Companies. Her repeated attempts to convince Ebby to participate in a biographical venture were met with polite replies by Ebby explaining that her story had already been told many times in several newspaper and magazine articles. Mary Frances finally prevailed, and Ebby's close friends and associates were pleased to contribute to the project.

In addition to Mary Frances, the following individuals shared hours of stories and recollections about Ebby: Anne Anderson, Don Davis, Steve Durham, June Feltman, Randall Graham, Linda Jordan Hobbs, Dulany Howland, Jim Lamb, Mary Lou Muether, Petey Parker, Betty Turner, and Mary Vlamides.

A bittersweet moment of this project occurred in early 2007 when I interviewed Paul Hanson, Ebby's brother, who was ill with progressive supranuclear palsy but very much in possession of all his mental faculties. He spoke for more than three hours one evening about growing up with Ebby and watching, at first, and then later participating with her while she built her company. His stories of serving as a Marine in the South Pacific during World War II were fascinating. He was a member in good standing of our greatest generation. Paul passed away March 12, 2007.

A close second to Mary Frances in terms of her enthusiasm for this project was Milli Brown, publisher and owner of Brown Books Publishing Group. Senior editor Janet Harris turned a historical manuscript into a concise narrative. Less was definitely more in this situation. Thanks also to Latham Shinder for enhancing the narrations and polishing the rough edges. Kathryn Grant, Jessica Kinkel, and Bill Young handled scheduling, layout, and design with efficiency and style.

Telling the story of Ebby's life and career would have inevitably proceeded with or without me as the storyteller. I just happened to be in the right place at the right time. Or more accurately, my wife Mary was fortuitously positioned to suggest that I might be able to help with the project. Her encouragement and support enabled me to devote the time that Ebby's story deserves. I would also like to thank Randall Graham, Director of Marketing for Ebby Halliday Companies, for entrusting the project to me.

Finally, there is Ebby, with whom I was privileged to spend many hours listening to stories about the Arkansas hills, the Kansas plains, and Dallas real estate. If I have managed to convey even 25 percent of this magnificent lady's philosophy, attitude, and values, then I will consider the effort to have been successful.

Michael Poss

# FOREWORD

Football and real estate have a lot in common. Leadership matters. Ambition counts. Heart energizes. Ebby Halliday might have made a good quarterback. Her intriguing story reflects her ambition to achieve despite all obstacles, her great heart that led her to reach out to her associates and customers, and her leadership that made her a role model. Her steadfast strength and brilliance radiate from every page.

Ebby and I have several things in common. Neither of us is a native Texan, but we both got to Dallas as fast as we could, albeit years apart. Neither of us arrived with plans for starting real estate companies, but good fortune, good friends, and good economic conditions attracted us to the real estate business. We were both blessed with great teams. The ability to see opportunities where others see obstacles, to envision strategies that turn short-term gains into long-term success, and to cling to our core personal values is the basis for our professional conduct and is essential for both of us.

Although I chose the commercial real estate route instead of residential sales, both share the need for leadership. I saw many leaders in the United States Naval Academy, in the Vietnam War, and in the National Football League. All possessed a fierce loyalty and devotion to their associates, which was returned in kind. Ebby Halliday personifies the kind of leader who leads with her heart, her entrepreneurial business sense, and her unflagging energy to make her dreams for herself, her company, and her community come true.

Ebby's story weaves history, economics, politics, personal anecdotes, business lessons, and life principles into a chronicle of an extraordinary life set against a background of the business of real estate. And yes, from my perspective, I think Ebby might have made a good quarterback.

Roger Staubach
Executive Chairman, Americas, Jones Lang LaSalle
Member of the Pro Football Hall of Fame

# Preface

*Dear Family,*

*At age ninety-four, I would like to share some of my thoughts with you. I would like to encourage each of you to live full lives and to help others along the way. I read something this week that hit me squarely between the eyes. The sentence read, "I need to submit my resignation as master of my own universe." When I read that sentence, I realized that as good as I've had it—my faith, family, friends, and success in business—that perhaps even better things might have come my way had I had a deeper faith in God's power to direct my life—had I not felt the need to be master of my own universe.*

*Before I go on, let me say that a daily relationship with God, expressing gratitude for life and asking for His guidance, is the foundation for reaching your goals and living a happy, fulfilled life. Take a few moments each day to pray. A few moments at night to express gratitude to the real master of the universe.*

*Okay, here goes. What follows is my recipe for a meaningful life.*

*1. Maintain your health. With health, all things are possible. Smoking and alcohol endanger your life and the lives of others. Drugs will kill you and ruin the lives of your family as well.*

*2. Keep learning. Make the most of opportunities to learn. Go to college, take special courses, read, listen, observe, and get out there and participate.*

3. *Choose a career wisely. Try for something that makes economic sense but also something you enjoy.*

4. *Learn to communicate. I've found that speaking to groups, being able to lead group discussions, presiding at a committee meeting, and giving a testimonial at Sunday school has been enormously helpful in my business and social life.*

5. *Build your self-confidence. People are impressed by what they see, what they hear, and what they feel in your presence. Dress appropriately and be well-groomed at all times. Speak clearly using correct English and use your manners, "Yes sir" and "No ma'am." Leave people with a positive impression. Especially in sales meetings, focus on the client, make good eye contact, and show a genuine interest in their needs.*

6. *Create good business habits.*

7. *Observe company policies. Know and understand the company objectives. Be prompt. Keep a positive attitude.*

8. *Express gratitude by thanking people. "I am grateful" and "thank you" are two very important phrases. Remember them.*

9. *Contribute to your community. Choose one or two outside interests, a service club, a nonprofit organization, a sport, a choir, or a church, and get involved.*

10. *Choose your partner carefully. Be careful whom you date because that may be the person you marry. List your general criteria for a life-long partner and then take your time finding that person. Select a partner that fits your criteria.*

*Maurice Acers, my husband and the love of my life, was the match for me. He was fifty, and I forty-six when we met. We married seven years later. We both had careers and many interests, which we successfully combined. I relied on Maurice's judgment and learned much from him. I'm so grateful for the time we spent together. Maurice died in 1993. He left behind a long list of accomplishments and service to others. I recall a sign on his desk that read, "Do something for someone every day." I have tried my best to observe this simple message and I hope you will too. Maurice continues to live in the memory and hearts of those who benefited from his counsel, wisdom, and generosity. He was a great man and a true Christian.*

*Each of you is at a threshold in your life.*

*Our country too is at a threshold since the terrorist attacks of September 11, 2001. The United States of America is meeting this new challenge with a unity of resolve, patriotism, and prayer. I believe we will overcome. As you grow, I believe you will see America as the best, the freest, and the most honorable country in the world. Our great nation offers the most opportunities for young people like you. We encourage diversity of religion, of worship, and of customs. We all pray to the same God, though by many names.*

*As my life winds down and yours is just beginning, know that your families love you. We believe in you and hope your lives and futures will be everything you want them to be.*

*Remember that a higher being is the Master of our universe. Let God be your partner. Be kind to each other, and do something for someone every day.*

*Yours always,*
*Ebby*
*2005*

# CHAPTER ONE
## From Hats to Houses:
## Knowing Your Customer

Vera Lucille Koch had been thinking of changing her name for some time. Years earlier, she'd picked up the nickname "Ebby," a name she liked but let drop when she moved to Dallas to manage the ladies' hat department at the W.A. Green Department Store. After six years, she'd had enough. The time was right to strike out on her own, and "Ebby's Hats" sounded like a fine name for a boutique hat shop. A friend mentioned "Halliday" as a last name, and Ebby liked the ring of it. So in 1945, Vera Lucille Koch, the small town girl from Leslie, Arkansas, became Ebby Halliday, the millinery shop owner of Dallas, Texas, a woman who sixty-three years later would be recognized as one of Texas's most outstanding businesswomen, owner of the largest independently owned residential real estate services company in Texas, with annual sales of more than $4.8 billion.

As Ebby had hoped, the hat shop attracted a new set of customers, many of whom were upscale Neiman Marcus shoppers. Ebby had a flair for designing hats. Her hatmaker, Pearl Kemendo, had a talent for bringing those designs to life. Together, the two women made the boutique the place for custom ladies' hats. No style-conscious Dallas woman felt dressed without a soft brown cashmere cap, a mink pillbox, or a wool beret with silver studs to complement her outfit. Often the only way to get such a hat was to have it made, and Ebby had a couple of advantages — she made one-of-a-kinds, and she made them quickly. The combination was a hit with the Dallas social scene, and the small shop sold enough to make the new business viable.

Ebby's best customer was Virginia Murchison, whose husband took a shine to one of Ebby's more creative designs made of sculpted felt and feathers. Not so much the hat, but the skill and bravado it took to sell such a thing impressed Murchison. On a hot day in 1945, Clint Murchison said to his wife, "The next time you visit your friend who sells the crazy hats, ask her if she has any ideas how to sell my crazy houses."

Clint Murchison, Sr., was an oil magnate who had gotten his start in the 1920s, working the oil fields west of Fort Worth. By 1929, he'd formed a pipeline company to distribute natural gas throughout the Southwest. A year later Murchison, Dad Joiner, and H.L. Hunt began developing the East Texas oil fields—a region that turned out to be the largest and most prolific oil reservoir in the contiguous United States.

Clint Murchison invested some of his oil money in real estate, construction, and the production of heavy industrial building materials. In 1944, he got the idea to build houses out of products manufactured primarily by his own companies. The houses were made of insulated cement panels poured and cured at a nearby cement plant, hauled to the construction site, and put together one piece at a time.

The home prices were reasonable—$7,500 for the two-bedroom, $9,500 for the three-bedroom. The problem was that nobody was buying.

Virginia told Ebby, "My husband seems to think if you can sell hats, you can sell houses."

"He does, does he?"

"They're concrete boxes. It's no wonder he can't give them away."

"I don't know a thing about selling houses," Ebby protested.

"Come on, let's take a drive. You can see what you'd be getting yourself into."

Ebby was curious and agreed to tag along on the twenty-minute drive to Walnut Hill, a development in the far northwest corner of the city. At first sight, Ebby had a fair idea why the houses weren't selling. The houses were sterile, cold, and bare. They were more akin to tiny prisons than homes. Clint Murchison's concrete boxes needed lots of things, but none so much as a woman's touch.

# THINKING LIKE A CUSTOMER

What Ebby Halliday understood intuitively was that buyers make decisions emotionally. First they have a need. Then they look for ways to fill that need that are both practical and emotional. To offer customers only half the equation would not work. The most important buying decisions would be based on emotion, not square footage, insulation value, or creative construction techniques.

The Walnut Hill homes were practical, all right. In many ways, they were ahead of their time. The modular construction methods were innovative and cost-effective. The homes could be manufactured and put together faster than conventional homes. The concrete walls were especially energy efficient in keeping the Texas sun out and indoor temperatures moderate, if not exactly cool. What the homes lacked, as it took Ebby all of three seconds to figure out, was an emotional reason to buy.

On the ride back downtown, Ebby thought of ways to make the homes more presentable. "Virginia, I have some ideas. Do you mind if I call Clint directly?"

"Certainly. He'll be interested in your ideas."

On the phone with Clint, Ebby explained. "Buyers have no idea what they want until they see it. We have to give them a picture. What you've given them is the before. Our job is to show them the after, give them a better idea what the house will look like after they move in."

"What are you suggesting?" Clint asked.

"Drapes for one. Showcase the windows, or at least those in the living and dining rooms. Carpet on the floor. If not carpet, how about a few rugs?"

4

"Is that all?"

"No, that's not all. We need furniture. A nice wooden Salem table, one that's not too big, and a few Windsor armchairs for the dining room. A settee for the living room. And the yards. I'd plant a few shrubs out front. Some grass for a lawn, no matter how small. Perhaps a little more paint on the front of the house to get away from the institutional feel."

"That's quite a list," Murchison said. "But okay. I'll have my foreman give you a call. You tell him what you want done. We'll fix up one house. If it sells, I'll pay you the standard commission. With any luck, we can decorate one at a time and go from there. One last thing. You'll need to get your real estate license."

## TAKING INITIATIVE

Ebby didn't ask about the standard commission. She didn't ask how to get a real estate license. She didn't ask about contractors, paint color, drapery fabric, carpet durability, or azaleas versus tulips. Clint Murchison was her new customer, her new client, and clients shouldn't have to explain her job to her, even if she'd never done it before. What she did was take initiative.

Another aspect of knowing her customers would be evaluating their expectations and understanding just how much or how little initiative would be required to meet those expectations. Her new client was looking for initiative, and Ebby had it by the bushel full. She grew up in an era when initiative and inventiveness were often all she had to work with.

Ebby Halliday was born on March 9, 1911, in the little town of Leslie, Arkansas. Three years later, her father, Louis Koch, was killed in a railroad accident. Her mother, Lucille, and Ebby's older brother, Raymond, and younger sister, Virginia, moved in with her grandparents, the Reverend James Mabrey and his wife.

In 1918, her mother married Fred Bigler and moved her small family to his farm near Gypsum, Kansas. The move from the Arkansas Ozarks to the Kansas prairie provided an enormous surprise. Gone were the apple and peach orchards, the blueberry and raspberry patches. In their places were fields of dull brown wheat and silky corn. The Bigler farm consisted of 640 acres of pasture, with dense thickets of cluster elm, post oak, and blaze maple; a clapboard farmhouse, barn, and smokehouse; and grain silos, a chicken coop, and lots of dogs and cats.

The house had a wide front porch with a hole cut into the pine floorboards. The hole allowed a bucket, connected to a chain and hand crank, to descend into the ground and draw water from the well. The Bigler house was lit with carbide lights with a tin concave reflector and clunky valves on the side to control the flow of acetylene gas.

There were lots of new chores but none bigger than sweeping scads of silty dust from the house. Given that the doors and windows stayed open most of the year and the maddening prairie wind blew continuously, keeping the ominous piles of dust at bay was a real calling. There was no end to the cooking, cleaning, washing, tending the enormous garden, grooming the orchard, and preparing for the upcoming wheat harvest. No chore was ever complete, no obligation ever fully finished. Something always needed to be done, or done better. Farm life was dirty, hard, and good for a young woman's character. Ebby thrived. She was creating habits that would last a lifetime.

Ebby knew all she needed to know about taking initiative. About selling houses, she had a lot to learn. Intuitively, however, she knew one thing—real estate would be a full-time business, and she wanted nothing distracting her from her new profession. The minute she received the offer to take over sales of the cement homes, she sold 100 percent of the ownership of Ebby's Hats to Pearl Kemendo, her hatmaker. The deal did not require any up-front cash, and Pearl could make payments on the buyout from the profits of the store. It was a great deal all around.

Ebby moved immediately into one of the box houses and used it as her sales office. Dressing up the interior was a cinch. She'd been through the process a year earlier with her new hat shop. With a few telephone calls, she lined up a landscaping firm, a carpet layer, and a painter. When the foreman finally called, she told him his only obligation was to unlock the house each day and pay the contractors.

She picked up a license application from the Texas Real Estate Commission. No test. As long as she wasn't a convicted felon and had a pulse, she'd receive her license in a few weeks. The fee to become an agent was three dollars. Anyone not working for a broker needed a broker's license instead. So Ebby paid five dollars and became a broker.

She learned that the commission was typically 6 percent, split evenly between the listing broker and the selling broker. Ebby would earn a commission of $285 on her first house. If she repeated the process a few times a month, she would earn serious money, considerably more than she made working at the hat shop.

Three weeks later, Ebby Halliday made the call to Clint Murchison.

"Sold," she told him.

"Already?"

"We have a contract on the Almazan Drive property."

"Think you can do it again?" he said.

"I've already scheduled the contractors."

"What if I said thanks but no thanks?"

She wasn't sure if he was joking with her, if this was his way of negotiating better terms, or if maybe he just wanted to see what she would say. Ebby sensed a pause was often the most powerful close.

"The homes on Bolivar and Cortez," Murchison said. "Let's sell those next."

In addition to managing the contractors, Ebby developed a marketing and advertising plan—printed brochures listing the features and price, banners and balloons for open houses, local contacts to spread the word, and a small advertising budget for newspaper ads. Each month she sold more houses, and business continued to grow. The challenge was how best to manage her scarcest resource—time. She would soon solve that problem by enlisting others to work with her.

## ATTRACTING CUSTOMERS

In December, Bill Muether and his brother-in-law, Gordon Abbott, skipped church to go quail hunting near the Walnut Hill development. The two had not hunted in Walnut Hill for years. When they arrived, they hauled out the shotguns, let the bird dogs out of the pickup, and headed across a field to a stand of trees. The dogs kept pace but never stopped to point. Either something was wrong with the dogs' noses or something had happened to the habitat. They reached the stand of trees and stopped. The two men stood gaping at what used to be untouched woodlands.

A new housing development had wiped out the trees on the backside of the woodland.

Bill yanked off his shooting gloves and crammed them into a pocket of his vest. The hunting trip was ruined. Their quail refuge was gone. They hadn't fired a shot. The pair stared across a newly paved street into the housing development. Gordon squinted at the new homes.

"Whaddaya looking at over there?" Bill asked.

"I'm not sure," Gordon said.

"Do you need the glasses?"

"No. It looks like a cute brunette wearing a housecoat and high heels."

Bill's eyes weren't too good. He glanced at the houses. "You're putting me on, right?"

"She's unlocking the front doors to the houses."

"Well, I'll be," Bill said.

The apparition disappeared. With their hunting trip all but over, the two men walked into the street with their shotguns and bird dogs in tow. Many of the houses were finished but vacant. They noticed a sign in one of the yards. It said, "Open." They tied the dogs to a post, kicked the mud off their boots, and eased inside. A brochure listed the prices, number of rooms, and names and style of appliances. It listed the broker, Ebby Halliday REALTORS®, along with her picture.

"That's her," Gordon said.

"How come you reckon she was wearing a housecoat?"

"Maybe I was seeing things."

"Well, were you?" Bill said.

Gordon shook his head. "Let's take a look around."

After a brief look at the house, the pair headed back to the truck and home. After hearing about the morning's adventure, Bill's wife, Mary Lou Muether, and her sister, Louise, decided it'd be worth the trip to see the houses and meet the real estate broker. By the time the couples arrived at the subdivision, the place was covered in balloons. The house was meticulously landscaped and the lawn freshly cut. Inside, the early-American furniture reminded Bill of farm living and big families and comfortable settings—a handcrafted library table in the entry, a large drop-leaf table and chairs in the dining room, and a Windsor rocker and settee in the living room. The woodsy furniture and its arrangement had a soothing earthiness to it. Draperies softened the bare walls and partially covered the industrial-style window casements. The main room was a thirty-foot combination living room and dining room. At one end, a door led to the kitchen where Ebby had baked fresh gingerbread cookies.

After a well-timed interlude so they could soak up the atmosphere, a petite brunette appeared.

"Hello," she said. "I'm Ebby Halliday. Thank you for stopping by. Let me tell you about the home."

Five minutes later, the men were hooked. Reeling in Mary Lou and Louise took a bit longer.

This house belonged to Ebby, she told them, but there were plenty of others available. The developer planned to build fifty-two homes in total. There were two floor plans: the two-bedroom and the three-bedroom. Louise and Gordon chose the house next door. Mary Lou and Bill selected the house two doors over. The couples moved into their new homes in less than a month.

Ebby and Mary Lou became good friends and even began showing homes together. At times when Ebby was busy with a buyer, Mary Lou gabbed with other prospects so they couldn't get away. The two made a good team. It was obvious to Ebby that Mary Lou was an asset. She suggested that Mary Lou get her real estate license.

"I couldn't," Mary Lou said.

"You can do anything you set your mind to."

"I've never held a real job in my life."

"Tell me you don't like what you're doing here with me."

"I do like it. But I don't even know how to fill out a contract."

"I can teach you the paperwork. What I can't teach is the way you connect with people, the way you make eye contact, how you make people feel comfortable and get to know them in a matter of minutes. Join me, Mary Lou. Let's do this together."

Mary Lou Muether accepted the challenge and became the first employee of Ebby Halliday Realtors.

## ANTICIPATING THE MARKET

Ebby did not know a thing about predicting housing market fluctuations in the mid-1940s; however, she did have a knack for anticipating the growth in population and amending her sales strategies to meet that new population's needs. In 1947, the housing market was influenced by a handful of drivers: the economy, available units, price, financing options, interest rates, home buyer disposable income, and demographics. Many of these were favorable to Ebby's emerging real estate business, but none so much as the growth in population.

World War II had been over for a year and a half, and veterans were returning home to Dallas by the boatload. Some planned to get married. Others searched for new jobs. And a disproportionate number wanted to buy a home, thanks to the GI Bill. In practical terms, the GI Bill gave returning veterans a wide range of benefits including one year of unemployment payments, subsidized college tuition and living expenses for students, and zero-down loans to buy homes and start businesses.

By anticipating the market of returning veterans, Ebby was well ahead of the learning curve in understanding the often complex requirements for helping veterans qualify for government-guaranteed home loans. She was also able to amend her sales approach. The new sales script went something like this: Given that buying a home required no money for a down payment, given that interest rates were low and that monthly mortgage payments were equally low, renting simply did not make sense. The question was not whether to buy, Ebby told veterans, but where. And she had just the location.

Ebby did what she always did, decorated a home, showed buyers her Walnut Hill inventory, mentioned the features, and filled out the paperwork. Sales to veterans were so brisk that Ebby needed more agents and a formal office to handle the flow of people and transactions. Business was good, but moving from house to house was becoming a nuisance. So, she bought one of the fifty-two for herself on the southwest corner of Gaspar Drive and Marsh Lane, a main thoroughfare to town, and turned it into an office and her personal residence. Even the combination office/residence was soon overrun with activity. However, with only a few unsold houses left in the subdivision, she would soon need more inventory.

It didn't take her long to solve both problems almost simultaneously. A cornfield across Marsh Lane provided the answer for more inventory. Ebby participated in a sale of the acreage to George Mixon, Sr., a real estate developer who carved up the property into individual lots and found two young home builders—Dave Fox and Ike Jacobs—to begin building houses. The pair would later form Fox and Jacobs and become one of the largest homebuilders in the country. The new frame houses trimmed with brick sold for $12,000 and $13,000 for the two- and three-bedroom models.

The problem with the overcrowded office/residence was solved by another real estate developer, H. Leslie Hill, who had built a new shopping center between the southern boundary of the Murchison houses and Northwest Highway. Ebby decided that it was finally time for a proper real estate office. In a bold move, she closed the office on Gaspar Drive, opened her first commercial office, and put up a new sign: Ebby Halliday Realtors.

# CHAPTER TWO
## Promoting a Dream

Ebby Halliday Realtors' new location was a shopping center on the corner of Northwest Highway and Marsh Lane. The office was just south of the Walnut Hill housing development, and coincidently, the same slice of land on which Bill Muether and Gordon Abbott hunted quail years earlier. Dallas was growing, and Ebby's business would grow with it.

The harder Ebby worked, the luckier she got. In 1949, she got a call from John Murchison, Clint Murchison's oldest son, and

Harold Volk. John was well aware of the challenges of selling his father's concrete houses. He was equally aware of Ebby's real estate successes. He believed she would be a perfect candidate to spearhead a project for the Dallas Citizens Council. The Council's goal was to promote the City of Dallas. One way to do that was to convince established businesses to relocate to Dallas. Dresser Industries, a company with close ties to Clint Murchison's oil and gas operations, had recently agreed to move its headquarters from Cleveland to Dallas.

John wanted to know if Ebby could help. Dresser executives needed homes, and he wanted Ebby to shoulder the responsibility of finding those homes.

"What do you say?" John asked.

"I'll do it," Ebby said.

John Murchison had just offered Ebby her dream job, helping Dresser executives to relocate to her fair city.

Dresser Industries came to prominence in the late 1800s when Solomon Robert Dresser created an oil drilling component called a "packer" that separated oil and water underground. In 1885, the company designed a coupling to join pipes in such a way as to eliminate leaks of natural gas. The coupling was an oil and gas sensation. For the first time, the Dresser coupling allowed long-range, safe distribution of natural gas from the oil fields to far-flung cities. The company prospered and quickly expanded. Dresser Industries went public in 1928 with the help of an investment banker named Prescott Bush, father of George H. W. Bush, the forty-first president of the United States, and grandfather of George W. Bush, the forty-third president. Prescott Bush served as a director of Dresser Industries for the next twenty-two years.

After accepting John Murchison's invitation to help, Ebby first took on the duty of finding a home for Dresser president and chief executive officer Neil Mallon. Thirty-three-year-old Mallon was a contemporary of Prescott Bush at Yale University and a fellow 1917 inductee into the secret society, The Order of Skull and Bones. In 1948, Mallon gave George H. W. Bush his first job after graduation from Yale. Later, George H. W. Bush, his wife Barbara, four-year-old George Walker, and an infant daughter moved to Midland where the senior Bush ran the West Texas operations for Dresser.

When Ebby first met with Neil Mallon, he had a list of requirements. At the top of the list were at least two full-sized tennis courts. Mallon, a bachelor, had invited his recently widowed sister, Hannah, and her four children to live with him. The entire family played tennis. Locating a home inside Dallas with two tennis courts proved impossible. However, Ebby did uncover a rambling house on twenty-two acres in a nearby suburb, where Mallon could build all the tennis courts he wanted.

After Mallon and family moved in, Hannah started an informal tennis club consisting mostly of friends. The club included Ebby, who could cover the court but was not, by her own admission, a gifted player. Over the years, Ebby frequently visited the Mallon household and often spoke with members of the Bush family as they stopped in to see "Uncle Neil" on their way through Dallas.

The Mallon home sale was a success. Ebby did her job well, and the Dresser management team took notice of her hard work. The result was more Dresser relocation work and more word-of-mouth advertising. The Mallon home was pricy, and such a sizable sale put Ebby's competitors on notice that her new firm did more than just sell cement boxes. Ebby Halliday Realtors was suddenly thrust into the big leagues.

## SELLING CLOVERINE SALVE

Selling came naturally to Ebby. Part of the reason was that she was driven by a deep-rooted sense of purpose. Even as a young girl, she understood the need for purpose, the need to have goals and objectives outside herself, a need to increase the value in life and the value in the lives of those around her. More than any other character trait or guiding principle, having a sense of purpose could get her past the hard times and keep her focused on accomplishing dreams.

In 1922, eleven-year-old Ebby lived on the Bigler farm with her family. By then her brother Raymond had abandoned school and committed himself to the family farm. Raymond's decision helped with the workload, but it couldn't help combat the tide of unforeseen and negative influences. That year wheat prices fell to ninety-four cents a bushel. This sort of fall in prices was counterintuitive. With the farm's output steady and statewide production down, everyone expected wheat prices to go up. They didn't.

Ebby sensed something was wrong. This was the second year in a row that wheat prices had slipped. Each year the farm took more work yet produced less profit. Finances were a strain on the family, and her mother and Mr. Bigler could not hide their disappointment. The family had enough money for the coming year, but spending would be tight.

An avid reader, Ebby was flipping through a magazine and spotted a catchy advertisement for Cloverine Salve. The ad displayed the top of a round tin in black-and-white with little clover leaves around the perimeter of the tin. Cloverine Salve, the ad claimed, was highly recommended for sores, ulcers, chapped hands, sunburns, and sore or aching feet. The salve was nothing less than a medical ointment miracle. And the profit earned from selling tins to friends and neighbors was equally impressive.

Ebby had a problem and had just stumbled upon the solution. The problem was that her family needed money, not so much for necessities, but for those small niceties that put a smile on her mother's face. The solution was to help by selling salve. She was almost certain none of the local stores sold the salve, but even if they had, that wouldn't have dissuaded her. Ebby had a better idea: selling door-to-door. So she placed an order for a dozen tins of Cloverine Salve. She would sell each tin for a few cents over her cost and pocket the profit. Her overhead was almost nothing. Old Deck, her pony, was her main source of transportation, and he required only oats, hay, and water, all in abundant supply on the farm.

A brochure arrived with her first order of Cloverine Salve. The leaflet included a short course in selling. She read and practiced all the steps, but it was the last step, a reminder really, that caught her attention: remember to ask for the sale. She repeated the sentence in her head as she approached each farmhouse. "Remember to ask for the sale. Remember . . . " It worked. Ebby sold the tins almost as fast as she could gallop Old Deck from farmhouse to farmhouse.

## GETTING AN EDUCATION

Once the summer was over, Ebby returned to the one-room schoolhouse known as Bethel 75, which housed grades one through eight, all of which were taught by one teacher. She worried that her Cloverine Salve sales and delivery hours would be cut short, thus limiting her sales. As it turned out, the schoolhouse was a boon for business. Far from hurting sales, the schoolhouse served as her most effective distribution channel. Once she had pretty much knocked on every door in the surrounding area, most of her selling took place by word of mouth. She worked like this: Mothers sent an order for one or more tins of salve and some money to school with their children. The following day, Ebby brought the tins to school and sent them home with the kids. Sales slowly began to climb. At about this time, her mother gave birth to her fifth child, Paul Mabrey Bigler.

The new baby brought increased responsibilities. Whatever free time her mother had was now consumed caring for Paul. And Franky, Ebby's two-year-old younger sister, never ran short of demands. Her mother never said anything to Ebby directly; she didn't have to. Ebby set her Cloverine Salve business aside. Her purpose in selling the salve wasn't only for the money but also to help support the farm and to take some of the workload from her mother.

The family needed her hands-on caretaking skills more than it needed a few extra dollars in the cookie jar. So she spent her free time helping out around the house, doing chores her mother didn't have time for, watching after little Franky, doing whatever she could for her new brother Paul, completing her own homework, and attending school. All this extra effort at home resulted in less time to study. Conversely, her schoolwork improved. Thanks in part to the one-room schoolhouse, she had four-and-a-half years of overhearing older students' lessons. As a result, none of her lessons were new but sounded vaguely familiar. She kept her ears open, and the sixth, seventh, and eighth grades were a breeze. Consequently, she was able to spend a great deal of time in the back of the schoolroom reading from a selection of books, many of which were classics. She found time to read all the volumes in the makeshift library.

If only Ebby's success at school could have been duplicated on the farm. In the summer of 1923, wheat prices dropped again, this time to ninety cents a bushel. Then things got even worse. In the following years, Saline County was plagued by high winds, drought, and grasshoppers. Bad luck swept the county in droves. By the time prices slowly inched upward years later, wheat crops in the area had been wiped out. "Farming was a crapshoot," Mr. Bigler said often. The risks, the uncertainty, the natural disasters, these things weren't lost on Ebby.

Two years later, she graduated from eighth grade, along with her younger sister, Virginia, who had managed to get herself double-promoted during her stint at Bethel 75. Most of their friends were poor and stayed close to home. Most worked on family farms. A few got full-time jobs in town and lived at home. Ebby and Virginia, however, wanted more education. More education meant attending high school in Chapman, Kansas, about forty-three miles to the northeast.

Her mother, Lucille, had mixed feelings about sending her daughters to a high school so far away. Lucille understood the importance of a good education, but she was not emotionally ready for her Ebby and Virginia to leave home. After agonizing over what to do for a few days, Lucille acquiesced. She took the girls to Chapman for a visit. They traveled the chunky roads in the family automobile—an Overland. When they arrived, they found safe and clean accommodations with the postmaster of Chapman and his wife. A school bus gathered the rural children from their rural homes on Sunday afternoons for the trip to Chapman and returned them after school on Friday.

Ebby performed well in the ninth and tenth grades, but Virginia's attention was distracted by other pursuits. As a result, Ebby would proceed by herself to the last two years of high school in Abilene, Kansas. As she saw it, she would need to work part time during the week and all day on Saturdays to help pay her room and board, and she had a plan. Ebby thought she could handle a sales job, so she asked her mother to take her to the J.B. Case & Company Department Store in Abilene.

When they arrived, the manager recognized Lucille. "Welcome, glad to have you in the store. Can I help you find something?"

Lucille said, "This is my daughter. She'll be going to school here in Abilene for the next two years, beginning in the fall."

"Is that so?"

"I'm going to miss her." Lucille glanced away, trying to compose herself. Seeing Ebby only on weekends had been hard enough. But seeing her just during the holidays might be unbearable, she thought. Lucille stared at a dress hanging on display. She turned back to the manager. "My daughter would like a job."

"With J.B. Case, you mean?" the manager said. "I'm not sure we will have any openings in the fall. I wish I could help. But I don't . . . "

Ebby interrupted, "I'm good with people."

"How old are you?"

"Sixteen, sir." Ebby glanced at one of the clerks talking to a customer. "I know how to sell."

"You do, do you?"

She told several funny stories about selling Cloverine Salve from farm to farm. She smiled and looked him in the eye. She asked opened-ended questions. "If I were to work here, what responsibilities would I have?" She listened when the manager spoke and repeated what she believed were key aspects of the manager's business, things she had read in her Cloverine Salve brochure: display, customers, packaging, delivery, and profitability. This little bit of experience and Ebby's enthusiasm were enough to win him over.

"And you'll want to be paid, I suppose," he said.

"Not if you don't think I'm worth it," Ebby said.

The man didn't move. "When can you start?"

He agreed to make space for her when she arrived for school in the fall.

Ebby reached for his hand. "You won't be disappointed."

## LEADING THE WAY IN INFORMATION SHARING

The J.B. Case Department Store post was Ebby's first formal job. She was never afraid of firsts, never afraid of what was up ahead, so long as she was leading the way. After completing her first sale to the executive team at Dresser Industries, she soon experienced another first. Ebby Halliday Realtors was the first broker, along with a firm headed by a local broker named Guion Gregg, to complete a home sale using the new Dallas Multiple Listing Service.

The MLS system had been around since 1923 and was already operational in three hundred cities around the country. In Dallas, on the other hand, it had taken ages for brokers to warm up to the idea of sharing information. The MLS was basically a large book of homes currently for sale in the area. The book was only as good as the information that brokers and agents were willing to share. In other words, if the majority of real estate brokers didn't like the idea of sharing their home listings with other brokers, they simply didn't report the information to the Dallas Real Estate Board, which maintained the MLS, and the information never appeared in the book.

The benefit of the MLS was that it streamlined the house-hunting process. Using the MLS, sales agents had a complete listing of all the homes for sale within a buyer's area. The MLS saved time. Agents could read descriptions of homes to buyers over the phone. The buyers could then decide to visit the property or not.

The Dallas MLS was launched on Sunday, February 1, 1953. On Friday of that week, Ebby and another broker announced they had completed the first transactions initiated through the system. Ebby's first MLS transaction helped locate a house for Neil Mallon's administrative assistant, Ms. Dale Pitt. Ebby flipped through the MLS book, found several possibilities, previewed the properties, and selected a short list to show her client, Dale, and her young daughter, Linda. The home Dale chose was a beautiful two bedroom near the Southern Methodist University campus. Dale and Ebby became good friends, and after retiring from Dresser a few years later, Dale got her real estate license as an agent for Ebby Halliday Realtors. Today, Linda and her husband, Jim Hobbs, are agents with the company, and Ebby counts them among her close friends.

# PLANNING FOR GROWTH

Ebby's dream wasn't just to sell houses, but to positively influence people's lives. One way to influence as many people as possible was to grow her business. The 1950s was a time of exceptional growth for Dallas, and Ebby's business kept pace. Sales came from a range of sources and influences: Dresser Industries relocating its corporate office to Dallas, new homes and small housing developments popping up across North Dallas, Ebby's growing list of contacts, and implementation of the Dallas MLS. All played a part, and all created enormous opportunities for new sales and the need for new agents. By the summer of 1953, Ebby had thirteen agents. A second commercial location was clearly needed. She had opened her first location to keep an eye on what Ebby considered "her territory," the Walnut Hill subdivision, and had chosen office space immediately south of the development.

That office was now bustling with agents, staff, and activity. At this point, Ebby was faced with a decision. Should she take more space adjacent to her existing office or open a second freestanding office? The second office would require more overhead: telephones, typewriters, filing cabinets, and other items. A second office meant more support personnel. However, eight years had also taught her the enormous value of having a visible, accessible, and comfortable location for her customers, especially her builders. The value of a new location outweighed the costs of additional overhead and staff. The only question was where to locate the new office.

"Location, location, location" as a real estate mantra first appeared in the *Washington Post* real estate section on March

30, 1952. The headline read: "What are the three most important considerations of the wise home investor?" The snappy response in bold type read, "Location, location, location."

Had the author, no doubt a lowly copywriter for the paper, been able to copyright this little gem, he might have retired comfortably without ever writing another word. Ebby took the advice to heart and chose the best location available. Ebby Halliday Realtors' newest office was located a quarter mile south of the intersection of two state highways. State Highway 289, known mostly as Preston Road, ran north almost to Oklahoma and south to downtown Dallas. State Highway Loop 12, known as Northwest Highway in the northern part of Dallas, circled the city.

Where Preston Road and Northwest Highway crossed, rooftops were quickly replacing cotton fields. The town of University Park was located thirty feet to the south and twenty feet to the east of the new office. University Park, named because its boundaries encompassed Southern Methodist University, and neighboring town Highland Park formed an affluent enclave known as the Park Cities.

The location of these two towns is an anomaly in modern city planning. Dallas is like a doughnut with the Park Cities as the hole. This so-called "hole in the doughnut" had been a source of distress for Dallas city leaders for years. In 1945, the citizens of Dallas, Highland Park, University Park, and Preston Hollow, another nearby independent community, went to the polls to vote on annexing or including these towns into the City of Dallas. Preston Hollow passed the measure, but the vote failed in the Park Cities. The following day—a Sunday—the Dallas City Council met in a special session and agreed to annex all of the remaining unincorporated areas surrounding the Park Cities, thereby freezing the boundaries of these tiny landlocked towns forever. Together, Ebby would find them to be some of her most fertile real estate markets.

Referring to the new Ebby Halliday Realtors' location as an office was somewhat charitable. In fact, the office was a converted builder's shed, positioned between two other sheds still in use by builders constructing houses within University Park. Selecting her office sites close to new home developments had proven advantageous in the past, so it was worth another try.

Within months, the activity and number of transactions of the Preston Road office had eclipsed those of the first office, which by this time had moved four miles north to a location on Forest Lane. The city continued to stretch north, and Ebby wanted to be at the center of that expansion. The intersection of Preston Road and Northwest Highway turned out to be the epicenter of home sales in the Dallas area during this time. The combination of building activity within University Park and the northern section of Dallas, plus the normal turnover within the nearby town of Highland Park, provided the staff with more than enough opportunity to establish a thriving operation. The new office was accessible and brought walk-in home buyers looking for help. More agents were added, and soon even more space was needed. Two years later, in 1955, the office moved to larger quarters, this time to a location on Northwest Highway, a quarter mile west.

Ebby's marketing activities did not stop with well-located offices. Now was the time to take her dream and her company to a new level—television.

# CHAPTER THREE
## Advertising the Four M's

Television advertising of the 1950s wasn't a whole lot different from advertising today. Commercials were black-and-white and the graphics cartoon-like by today's standard, but the purpose hasn't changed: to inform potential customers about products and services. Ebby's purpose was to showcase her growing real estate company and to sell houses. If television worked for selling gasoline and cornflakes, she reasoned, why not houses?

Ebby jumped into TV by airing a series of one-minute advertisements. The ads ran twice a day for twenty days, forty in all. Because the commercials were live, Ebby made forty trips to and from the television studio in downtown Dallas, a long haul twice a day, given the growing automobile traffic in Dallas. Ebby's personality and wide smile made her a natural for TV. She appeared dressed in a cream-colored dress and black pillbox hat, describing the homes pictured on the screen, and giving directions to one of her local real estate offices. She closed each commercial by inviting buyers to stop by and say hello. The ads worked, sales jumped, and new home listings steadily increased.

## SHOWMANSHIP COUNTS

Television advertising was and is about more than communicating benefits and features. Television is also about showmanship, and Ebby was no stranger to showmanship. Her stepfather, Fred Bigler, was himself a showman of sorts.

Ebby's last year on the Bigler farm was the same year drought and grasshoppers destroyed the harvest. In 1925, after cutting and binding what was left of the wheat crop, Fred Bigler simply piled the parched stalks in a roadside ditch to dry up and blow away. No harvest meant no revenue. With little left in the bank, Fred and his wife, Lucille, had to find another source of income.

Before committing to farming, Fred Bigler had tried his hand at a long list of other trades, most poorly paying, go-nowhere jobs. However, one had a slim chance of earning the Biglers a pot full of cash—professional wrestling. Until the 1920s, wrestling was viewed as a legitimate sport, second only to baseball in popularity.

Fred Bigler was athletic and exceptionally strong. He was fast. His physical prowess was admired throughout the county.

Lucille hated the idea. Professional wrestling sounded seedy. Fred could get hurt, and he would be away from the farm for long stretches. After putting off a decision for weeks, Lucille finally agreed; they didn't have much choice. Falling wheat prices and bad weather had driven many farmers in Saline County from their farms. Jobs were scarce, and the family needed an income, no matter the source.

Big Fred Bigler spent the next few weeks getting into shape. The rigors of farm life had kept him in peak physical condition. All he needed was to work on his wrestling moves—chokeholds, body slams, face busters, pile drivers—and he would be ready for the ring.

In his youth, Fred Bigler had been a great wrestler. Now, a few years older, he might only be good, but more importantly, he was handsome and muscular. Best of all, he was a showman, and showmanship filled seats. The spectacle wasn't about being the most adept wrestler. In the early 1920s, promoters began deciding who won and who lost. What Fred had going for him was a natural flair for entertaining audiences.

The transition for Ebby's family, especially her mother, would not be easy. The family's nearest neighbor was a mile away. With Ebby's brother, Raymond, off looking for work and Ebby herself leaving for school in a few weeks, her mother Lucille would be left with an eleven-year-old, a four-year-old, and a two-year-old to care for, not to mention a large crumbling farmhouse and a square mile of farmland that needed tending. Ebby and her mother were good at adapting to change; having a professional wrestler for a father and a husband was a change they would survive. By the time Ebby left for high school that summer, Fred Bigler was busy wrestling in towns all across the Midwest.

## MOBILIZING A TEAM

Like her stepfather, Ebby also had a flair for entertaining audiences. While opening new offices and producing her television ads, Ebby had taken on a handful of board positions, including director of the Dallas Real Estate Board. She spoke regularly at organization events and became a rising star on the statewide speaking circuit. In September 1952, she spoke to the Real Estate Board of Wichita Falls, Texas. Her talk was titled "How to Make Advertising Pay Sales Dividends," and she outlined her Four M's of Real Estate: merchandise, message, mobilization, and medium. *Merchandise* referred to having a saleable product. *Message* meant creating good ad copy. *Mobilization* was about getting the sales team out in the field to support that message. And finally, *medium* meant choosing the right ad media—classified advertising, television, billboards, and signage. Possibly more impressive than her content, Ebby dazzled the audience with her delivery. A follow-up article in the local newspaper described her as a "dynamic Dallas realtor," a woman who had founded a firm that had spectacular growth, six years running.

Ebby's speaking and board positions went hand in hand—the more she spoke, the more positions she was offered and accepted, and vice versa. What she discovered was that both the speaking circuit and the boardroom needed a female presence. Ebby soon set her sights on becoming a key member of the nation's largest real estate trade association, the National Association of Real Estate Boards, later to be renamed the National Association of Realtors®.

In the 1950s, the NAREB boards were composed almost exclusively of men. Twenty-eight years earlier, California had invited women to join the state association, not as members, but as associates of a newly formed Women's Division of the California Real Estate Association. Not all states and cities had a Women's Council. For example, Ebby's budding metropolis of Dallas didn't. Ebby believed that women were capable and qualified to take on greater leadership roles. She also believed in sharing information, an essential benefit of any trade organization. To that end, she decided to charter a Dallas chapter of the NAREB Women's Council.

She quickly mobilized her team by assembling eighty charter members for the inaugural meeting in September of 1954, the largest Women's Council ever formed. Ebby was elected president of the chapter, and the membership quickly grew to one hundred. The following year, in January, she was named governor of the 12th District of the Women's Council, which covered Texas and Louisiana. This new position marked the beginning of a speaking career that would have her crisscrossing the nation for years to come.

## MAKING WORK A HABIT

Since early childhood, Ebby loved work. After the summer of 1927, she was off to Abilene to attend the last two years of high school and work at the J.B. Case Department Store. When Lucille and Ebby arrived in Abilene, Helen, her new roommate, had already arrived. Helen was friendly and knew the school system, a godsend for sixteen-year-old Ebby.

First on her mind was to check on the job the manager at the J.B. Case Department Store had promised her three months earlier. Her future depended on getting this job. If he changed his mind, she could not afford the room and board, couldn't afford high school. When the doors opened, she found the manager.

"Yes, of course," the manager said. "I said I'd make an opening for you, and so I will."

"When can I start?"

"School begins in a few days. Is that right?"

"I can start any time." Ebby looked the manager in the eye. "Right now, if you like." She glanced at several of the customers, women in loose-fitting, calf-length dresses. "I am good with ladies' fashion."

Three women strolled down the aisle. The manager said, "Welcome, ladies. May I help you? We have some beautiful new satin gowns, crepe-de-chines, silks, crepes, and chiffons. Just over there."

The women smiled and shuffled off in the direction he indicated.

"Today would be better," Ebby said. "To start, I mean."

"Assertive, aren't you?"

"I want this job more than anything."

"I'm thinking next week. I'll need time to put together a schedule. Let the staff know what's what."

"My landlord, Judge Crane, do you know him?"

"Everyone knows Judge Crane, yes."

"He dropped me off this morning, and I have nowhere to go until he picks me up at five-thirty. I'd be obliged if you let me work in between."

"Like I said, you're not shy. I'll give you that." He called an impromptu meeting of the sales staff in the ladies' department and announced the addition of their new part-time sales clerk. Ebby felt both relieved and exhilarated.

At sixteen, Ebby settled into a life full of activity and pace. School began at eight, finished at two-thirty. She worked at the store until five-thirty, caught a ride home with Judge Crane, ate dinner with the judge and his wife at six, and studied until her eyes got tired. On Saturdays, she worked from nine to five. On Sundays, she attended the Methodist church with Helen.

Keeping to her busy schedule was exactly the discipline she needed to get through the tenth grade, which was harder than she expected. She had reports and compositions to write, research to analyze. Arithmetic suddenly turned into algebra. Fortunately, history was still history, just more of it to read about.

The following summer she worked full-time at the store while continuing to rent a room from the Cranes. Ebby's duties included the piece goods department. Stacking and unstacking bolts of material was hard work. A lady approached her one day and asked for help finding material for a quilt. The woman pointed to a bolt of cloth. Ebby lifted the bolt from its shelf and placed it on the cutting table. The lady politely asked for a two-inch strip. Ebby cut the strip and returned the bolt. The lady pointed to another bolt and asked for another two-inch strip. She repeated the process a dozen times. The woman was making a flower garden quilt typically stitched together from scraps, but she had run out of scraps.

"I have seven sons," the woman said. "Arthur, Edgar, Dwight . . . "

"Seven?"

"They all went to Abilene High School."

"That's where I go," Ebby said.

"Several of the older boys are married now, starting families.

This cloth, it's for one of my grandchildren. I make all the grandchildren a quilt. Always have. Expect I always will."

The woman introduced herself.

Ebby smiled. "I recognize the name. In the trophy case at school. They have pictures of some of your boys next to the trophies."

"That's them," she said. "Good athletes, every one of them." She paid for the cloth and thanked Ebby for the help.

"It was nice to meet you, Mrs. Eisenhower."

As if Ebby wasn't busy enough, she planned to try out for the cheerleading team in the fall. She devoted all her free time to polishing her routines. She made the team, which added to her long list of commitments. She stayed up later and got up earlier. She completed her homework, worked at the store, practiced with the cheerleading team, and occasionally had time for a school function. When she graduated from Abilene High School in May 1929, it would be hard to imagine an eighteen-year-old who carried a heavier load than Ebby Halliday.

## GETTING OUT THE MESSAGE

Carrying a heavy load was what Ebby did best. As she crisscrossed the country giving speeches, she regularly spoke on the Four M's of Real Estate: merchandise, message, mobilization, and medium. Of the four, her overall theme was getting out her message. That message was not always overt; in fact, it was often implicit in the way she conducted herself, the way she worked, and her commitment to her customers, her business, and her real estate association. She believed in a strong work ethic. She believed that women could, and should, take on greater leadership roles. She believed that customers would trust her only when she took the time to listen. And she shared these ideas both in her speeches and by way of example in how she lived her life.

As governor of the 12th District of the Women's Council, Ebby was required to tour each of the NAREB offices in her district. The tour began in Beaumont, Texas, where she appeared on a panel to discuss real estate sales techniques. A week later, she spoke in Corpus Christi, Texas, at the Texas Real Estate Association on "Women in the Real Estate Profession." Two weeks later, it was a two-hundred-mile round trip to Waco, Texas, where she gave the same speech, and then another two-hundred-mile round trip to Tyler, Texas, for a repeat of her "Women in Real Estate" talk. On she went: Austin on Tuesday, Houston on Saturday, back to Corpus Christi in June.

That summer, Ebby made appearances in Houston, San Antonio, and Oklahoma City. An Oklahoma City reporter described her as a fiery little brunette from Dallas who set the Hotel Tulsa ablaze with her speech on "The Four M's of Real Estate." Two weeks later, she joined a delegation of seventy-five real estate professionals at the annual NAREB convention in New York City. She appeared on a Women's Council panel and was later chosen as a regional vice president for Texas, Louisiana, Arkansas, and Oklahoma.

In early 1956, she appeared in Beaumont for a real estate panel, in Oklahoma City and Tulsa for a pair of back-to-back seminars, and in Lubbock for the Texas Real Estate Association Women's Council convention. In addition, each year the Texas Real Estate Association sponsored workshops. That year Ebby and six men agreed to conduct the TREA workshops. Over a three-week period in September, they traveled to eight cities—Longview, Waco, Austin, Wichita Falls, Lubbock, San Angelo, Corpus Christi, and Harlingen—to deliver the workshops. A week later, Ebby was in Nashville speaking at the Tennessee Real Estate Association. In October, she spoke to professionals in Kansas, four days later to seminar members at the San Antonio Real Estate Board.

In 1957, the nominating committee of the Women's Council of the National Association of Real Estate Boards submitted Ebby Halliday for president of the council. Ebby's election marked the fastest climb ever to the presidency of the Women's Council, only two years after she chartered the Dallas chapter. In her address at the convention in St. Louis, she urged real estate professionals to render better service by expanding their personal knowledge of real estate and of human behavior. A blend of academic knowledge and personal experience was essential to success, she said. "Self-confidence, so necessary to a salesman, is earned through knowledge. And by self-confidence, I mean the kind so real and sure it enables you to grasp and never lose your buyers' point of view."

This level of self-confidence took focus. "Try this," she said. "Draw a mental curtain around yourself. Shut out the details of your own life. Instead, aim an imaginary spotlight on your customer. Become fully absorbed in your customer's point of view." She told the audience that this exercise would enable each of them to keep the correct mental attitude. This approach would automatically create an environment of mutual respect. "In fact, follow my advice and you might find it easier to get along with chronically disagreeable customers." Ebby's spotlight on her customers, friends, family, and association members made her instantly likeable and allowed her to build communities of like-minded people faster than just about any of her contemporaries.

## BUILDING COMMUNITY

Building community was fundamental to Ebby's way of thinking. Serving society was one of the implicit pillars of her work ethic and Ebby Halliday Realtors' mission: serve the client, serve the community, and serve the industry. Sharing her ideas, growing her own business, and encouraging women to get involved were all part of the same message, a message that had become clearer with each speech: improve your life by improving the lives of those around you.

As council president, Ebby traveled to Ardmore, Oklahoma, where she spoke about civic duty and volunteering. She told the crowd, "It is our duty and privilege as Realtors to get involved, to participate in the activities of our cities, and to help build our communities." Early in her career, Ebby displayed a genuine entrepreneurial spirit, a contagious spark of energy, and an unending devotion to her community and her industry. This commitment and energy kept her going when others might have chosen a slower pace.

In March 1957, she made a trip to Jackson, Mississippi, for a one-day real estate workshop. The topic, "Streamlining Your Office," included tips on recording new listings, choosing office locations, creating office layouts, keeping sales staff productive, and reaping the benefits of advertising. The material was pragmatic and useful. Next, she spoke in Kansas City at the annual Missouri real estate convention, then in Nashville and later in Little Rock. Having already seen enough snow as a child, Ebby headed for Connecticut in June for a two-week speaking tour, in which she dusted off "The Four M's."

Ebby was often the lone female speaker at these events. She was doing exactly what others said a woman couldn't do: creating a successful business; managing the daily grind of the speaking circuit; and focusing not on herself, but on her clients, her community, and her industry. She remained positive throughout this grueling schedule. Nothing was impossible. Once she accomplished a goal, she remained true to herself and her mission. Whenever possible, she helped others enjoy the same success.

After Connecticut, she returned home to review the company business. In addition to all the travel, she had opened a third office in the northeastern part of Dallas three months earlier. This new location was smack in the middle of a new housing boom north of the inner-city reservoir known as White Rock Lake. Consistent with her idea of sharing her successes, Ebby promoted assistant sales agent, Dorothy Walter, to manage the new office. Dorothy had gleaned the bulk of her management skills simply by listening and watching Ebby interact with customers and fellow professionals. Long before the notion of mentoring became a popular business buzzword, Ebby had initiated her own brand of management training. She surrounded herself with capable staff and then gave each member of her staff opportunities to take on greater leadership roles.

With key people managing the day-to-day activities of each of her offices, Ebby could focus on the big picture. A part of that picture was brand exposure. Ebby Halliday Realtors was still a young company, and Ebby wanted to boost the company's identity in the marketplace. One way to do that was to get out there and spread the word, one person or one group at a time.

Ebby discovered that day trips were as exhausting as overnight stopovers. Nonetheless, she tried to fulfill as many of the speaking requests as her calendar allowed. In July, she spoke at conventions in Louisiana and Oklahoma. In late August, she began the Florida Real Estate Commission lecture series in Miami. The Commission had designed a one-day lecture series entitled "Applied Real Estate Practices." The program consisted of presentations by two noted Chicago-area real estate brokers, a former general counsel of the commission, and Ebby. Once again, Ebby pulled out her "Four M's of Real Estate" speech and entertained her audience.

After Miami, she hopscotched the state—Miami to Tampa to Ft. Walton to Jacksonville—keeping her strenuous schedule, four cities in four days. After Jacksonville, she stopped in Myrtle Beach for a joint meeting of the real estate boards of South Carolina, North Carolina, Kentucky, Tennessee, and Virginia. She gave an impressive talk titled "The Realtor Is an Interpreter." Ebby told the audience, "It is important that we listen to our customers. Try your best to understand their words, or more importantly, their meaning. Keep in mind that it's not always possible for your customers to articulate exactly what they mean. It is your job," she said, "to ask questions, to uncover purpose, to determine the precise meaning, to understand fully your customer's wants and needs. Equally important is knowing what your customer is not saying." Ebby emphasized that asking questions is a good way to draw out a customer's thoughts, to get to the bottom of things, even if the answer is "no sale."

She returned to Dallas just long enough to rest and prepare for a round of speeches in the Great Lakes. In September, she spoke twice at the Michigan Real Estate Association convention in Grand Rapids. The first presentation, "The Impact of Women on the Real Estate Business," was described in the program as "open to all women realtors and saleswomen." With such a limiting endorsement, it's not surprising there wasn't a man in the room. Later in the day, Ebby gave a keynote luncheon address, her topic, "Streamlined Creative Selling." Days later, she gave the same luncheon address in McCall, Idaho, and then shuttled north and east to the Montana Association of Realtors annual meeting in Great Falls where she spoke twice on "Women in Real Estate."

Ebby's talk gave women hope at a time in the late 1950s when divorced and single working women were considered somewhat questionable. Ebby's approach was to educate women and give them an honest and professional way to earn a good living. She reminded the audience that clients are impressed by what they see when they look at you, what they hear when you speak, and how they feel in your presence. She often included an anecdote that put a humorous spin on the paternal attitude of the times. "I was invited to give a keynote dinner address at a recent state convention. The plane was late, and I rushed to the hotel, quickly changed, and hurried into the elevator. A group of delegates wearing name badges stood in the elevator next to me. I settled myself and asked if the convention was going well. One man frowned. He said, 'Up until tonight. Some woman is the speaker.' We exited the elevator, eased into the banquet room, and I took my seat at the head table. I glanced back at the man squirming in his seat."

# CHAPTER FOUR
## Smiling Works

In September 1957, Ebby spoke in Kentucky to the Women's Council of the Louisville Real Estate Board. She talked about understanding your personal sales style, adapting your sales behavior to each customer, and the power of that first customer contact. For example, she suggested several tips to handle incoming calls effectively: use a script, let others speak, intend to hear what others are saying, and never speak when others are talking. Her best advice, she told council members, was to make sure to have the right frame of mind when answering the phone. Displaying genuine enthusiasm when answering a phone projects personality, and the best way to display enthusiasm, she suggested, was to use a trick she applied in her own offices. Install a mirror directly opposite all staff members who answer the phones. On the mirror, in bold letters, write the word "SMILE." When people smile, they communicate confidence and friendliness. That simple reminder is all the encouragement most people need to sit taller, begin each call with a grin, and use a telephone voice that is both pleasant and persuasive.

Smiling worked, and Ebby had seen it in action. She had witnessed the results all her life. Just two years out of high school, in the summer of 1931, she reluctantly entered the local Miss Abilene beauty contest. She knew nothing about beauty pageants, but her co-workers at the J.B. Case department store encouraged her to enter. In fact, they selected a yellow bathing suit they thought would be a perfect outfit for the pageant. Ebby donned the suit, a cotton print with a square-bottomed overskirt, and liked what she saw. However, had she known that the format required contestants to participate in a parade, balancing atop a slow-moving flat-bed trailer in nothing but a bathing suit, she might have given the decision more thought. When the parade began, Ebby was there on the trailer in her form-fitting one-piece, waving her hand and giving the crowd that big Ebby smile.

Her friends stationed themselves at strategic locations along the parade route and cheered wildly. After the last truck passed the judges' stand, the contestants were assembled on the makeshift stage. Each contestant walked across the stage, stopped briefly to survey the crowd, and let loose a confident smile. That was all there was to it. The judges announced the second runner-up, the first runner-up, and with a flourish from the band, the master of ceremonies announced, "Ladies and gentlemen, the new Miss Abilene is Vera Lucille Koch!"

Winning the pageant was a thrill, but her enthusiasm for pageants didn't last. Ebby had other ambitions for herself and those around her.

## EMPOWERING WOMEN

What got Ebby genuinely excited was standing in front of an audience and sharing her thoughts and experiences. After delivering her "Smile" speech in Louisville, she traveled to Raleigh for the North Carolina Association of Realtors annual meeting, where she was the featured speaker. After Raleigh, she took a train to Philadelphia to give an after-dinner talk.

A week later, she spoke in Monroe, Louisiana, and again in Detroit, Michigan, at the "Industry-Wide Housing Conference and Salesman-Making Workshop." A flyer promoting the event described Ebby as the most dynamic, convincing, and inspiring speaker to grace the NAREB stage. Besides having the charm, the flyer said, Ebby Halliday has the poise, beauty, and ability to tell others how to succeed, because she has succeeded herself. The advertising promotion for the Detroit conference was effusive. The ad copy did everything but grab would-be conference goers by the arm and tug them through the doors. The advertisement described Ebby as a national speaker, a "keen observer of national trends, and a Realtor with her finger on the pulse of the nation." Miss this conference, the ad scolded, and "you'll regret it the rest of your life. Don't miss this dynamic fireball with a sales-inspiring punch that will send you out with a will to sell."

Ebby had burst onto the national real estate scene with a flair. Once there, she often used her newfound celebrity to speak directly to women. Her goal was to raise awareness about the benefits of a career in real estate. During an interview in Detroit, she explained why she believed women were well suited for the job. She said that real estate was a good business for women because it offered so many unique challenges. Selling real estate satisfied a desire to serve and to work with people. It allowed agents to show off a talent for advertising, to get involved with civic projects, and to help shape their communities.

Ebby added that women in real estate bring with them integrity and a social consciousness, an awareness of the problems that our society and local communities face on a day-to-day basis. She cautioned against underestimating the power of intuition. The selling process is about more than price, schools, and features. Selling often involves discovering what motivates each buyer. Intuition, more than any other character trait, is a valuable tool for unearthing that motivation, she continued. Ebby's women-centered speeches were intended to inform, motivate, and inspire women who were interested in supplementing their income and empowering their lives.

In late 1957, Ebby handed off the presidency of the Women's Council to her successor. During her address at the National Association of Real Estate Brokers annual convention, she spoke about her experiences as Women's Council president, the thousands of individuals she had met, the hundred thousand miles she had traveled, the sixteen state conventions she had attended, and the fifty or more presentations she had given during the year. Finally, she spoke of the gratification she gained from participating in community activities. It was a fitting conclusion to her tenure as council president.

This was her last appearance as council president and the beginning of a new phase of her speaking career. Her speaking schedule began in Wisconsin at a sales seminar sponsored by the Milwaukee Board of Realtors. A newspaper headline the next day read, "Real Estate's Glamour Girl Says 'Sensitivity' Sells Houses." Audiences took to Ebby for several reasons. She had a fresh and often brash delivery, and she had an empowering personal story to share. Her life included a fair number of hardships, and if she could overcome those hardships, so could others.

## SHOWING OFF THE MERCHANDISE

In 1930, when Ebby was nineteen, the Depression had finally crept its way across Kansas. The year had been unusually dry for farmers, but most in Abilene had made a wheat crop. The following year was different. Wheat was everywhere—in the grain elevators, on the ground, and littering the road. So much wheat meant good news for consumers and bad news for farmers. The oversupply forced prices down from 63 cents a bushel in 1930 to 25 cents a bushel in 1931. Kansas farmers went broke; many simply abandoned their fields.

Abilene was a farming community, and fewer farmers and their families meant fewer shoppers at J.B. Case department store. Shoppers quickly looked for cheaper goods elsewhere, turning from the medium-priced J.B. Case store to less expensive stores, such as J.C. Penney. Some families shopped only for essentials.

Others stopped shopping altogether, holding onto their money, believing the dollar would be more valuable in a few weeks or months as prices continued to fall.

Without customers, the manager at J.B. Case would be forced to fire staff. Once that happened, Ebby was in trouble. She needed a job, and Abilene didn't have a lot to offer. The following year, things got worse. Wheat prices dropped again, and the time was right for Ebby to make a move. The best time to find a department store job was the Christmas holiday season. She sat down with pencil and paper and planned.

She was leaving Abilene. That was settled. Just where she was heading was still up in the air. During her five years at the J.B. Case store, Ebby had heard countless stories from customers about The Jones Store in Kansas City, the biggest and best department store in the world, according to some. Any store that large must surely require hundreds of employees and would likely need additional sales help through the holidays. Ebby didn't have a whole lot of options. Kansas City it was.

Ebby thought things through. In addition to packing her travel bag, she loaded her trunk with the remainder of her belongings and left it neatly tucked away in her room. If she found a job, even a temporary one, it might be enough encouragement to send for the trunk.

The Jones Store was larger than she had imagined. The mixture of excitement and apprehension overwhelmed her. The store was like nothing she had ever seen, an emporium of crystal, china, silver, and lighting; it all glittered. The store carried a boundless variety of merchandise. It even had a pharmacy with patented medicines, drugs, and chemical products, such as insect killers.

She had one thing to do before proceeding to the personnel office. She wanted to get to know the merchandise in ladies' clothing. Once there, she found many of the brands and dressmakers she had been selling for years. Outfits with soft lines and tucks and pleats and drapes, full-skirted, romantic evening dresses, strapless and hoopskirted. She also found a wide range of colorful accessories. At J.B. Case, women's accessories had been black or navy. Here were pinks and blues and copper. She also became aware that despite the Depression, a fair number of shoppers were meandering through the store.

When she reached the personnel office, a crowd of young women filled the waiting room, sitting in wooden chairs and filling out job applications. Given the competition, her prospects looked scant. But, she hadn't come this far to give up. Ebby grabbed a form out of a nearby box and quickly filled in the information and underlined her experience with J.B. Case. The clerk took her application, gave her a number, and curtly asked her to take a seat. The process seemed hopelessly efficient. She waited and watched as a steady stream of applicants got up from their chairs, entered a room, and shut the door. Three minutes later, they opened the door and left the store. Whatever confidence they had going in had all but evaporated when they came out.

An hour later, Ebby entered the small office. A table and two chairs were arranged near the back wall. A dour-looking woman sat in one of the chairs. The woman didn't introduce herself. She motioned for Ebby to sit and scanned the application in her hand.

The woman said, "I am sorry, dear, but The Jones Store isn't hiring sales clerks at this time."

"I have other experience," Ebby said. "It's all there in my application."

"Hats," she said. "You've sold hats?"

"Hundreds of them."

"Tell me something about hats, dear."

"What would you like to know? I've sold Florentine, Austrian, perts, cocktail hats, and snoods. Last week, I sold a lamb chop hat to Mrs. Hackbarth. She lives in Solomon, not six miles away, but rarely comes to town. I sold a sporty tweed Cossack to Miss Darnell on Saturday."

The woman made a note on Ebby's application. She raised a hand, motioning her to stop.

Ebby said, "I sold two Victorian revival hats to Mrs. Lahey and a fruit basket hat each to the Oliphant sisters over in Moonlight."

"That's enough, dear."

"I have quite a bit of experience selling hats."

"I'm sure you do, dear."

"I didn't see the hat department when I strolled through the store."

"Our hat department is owned and managed by Consolidated Millinery. They lease space from us, and I happen to know they're looking for a sales assistant with experience."

"I would be grateful if you would pass my name along."

"I can do better. If you'll go downstairs to our basement, you'll find our hat department. Tell them Ms. Whitley sent you. They'll know what to do."

The job was a dream come true for the young girl from the hills of Arkansas by way of the plains of Kansas. By the end of the day, she had a full-time job in Kansas City, working in the finest department store in town. Her pay was a whopping ten dollars a week.

Ebby was a hit with Consolidated Millinery. Hat sales quickly improved. She didn't understand the reason. On the other hand, Miss O'Shea, her manager, did. Miss O'Shea asked Ebby to try on a few hats. Ebby had a way of making any hat look attractive. She had pleasant features, a beautiful oval-shaped face, and a broad smile. When these were combined with one of Consolidated Millinery's hats, the merchandise began to move. If a customer wanted to try on a particular hat, Ebby slipped the hat on to indicate just how it should be worn. This little bit of salesmanship gave customers ample opportunity to admire the combination, Ebby's face and the hat itself. If the hat looked good on Ebby, then surely it would look just as good on them.

Ebby had a natural style and finesse for dealing with customers. According to Miss O'Shea, Ebby had a way of "getting along."

## GETTING ALONG

Ebby had a few golden rules for selling—be honest, touch people's lives, look at people when you talk to them, don't criticize the competition—but no rule so powerful as getting along with people. Getting along meant encouraging home buyers to make good decisions, showing kindness, praising, and being concerned for others' feelings. Getting along meant taking a genuine interest in people, gaining their confidence, and keeping an open mind. Getting along with people was one of the key skills that allowed Ebby to connect with hundreds and thousands of people throughout her career.

In 1958, she spoke in Detroit at two newly formed chapters of the Women's Council. She told the audience that becoming a success in real estate had several requirements. The primary requirement was just four words: "Get along with people." Human relations, she told the gathering, should be the number one concern of everyone selling real estate.

Getting along with people had always come easy to Ebby. Her manager at The Jones Store, Miss O'Shea, had spotted this character trait early. Ebby urged office and sales managers in the audience to do the same, to look for an ability to get along in their own staff. "Once you find it, encourage it, nurture it," she said. There was more to selling than getting along, of course, but this single quality couldn't be overrated. Over the years, Ebby had turned getting along into an art. Customers left Consolidated Millinery feeling better about themselves. Buying a hat was about style and fashion. It was also about looking and feeling different. Women in the 1930s who bought hats wanted to give off an air of being interesting and sophisticated, and Ebby had a way of helping women find the hat for just such a feeling.

By all accounts, Ebby's hat sales should have declined. The national unemployment rate in 1934 was a devastating 21.5 percent, nearly the highest in the nation's history. The country was suffering, yet Ebby's hat sales and her personal financial situation continued to improve. While she had received moderate pay increases the previous year, she was still a weekly employee. Midway through the year, Miss O'Shea promoted her to a monthly salaried position and gave Ebby a raise to $75 a month. Ebby was ecstatic.

"I can't tell you what this means to me," Ebby said.

"Don't thank me. You earned it," Miss O'Shea told her.

Consolidated Millinery, like other profit-centered companies during the Depression, was not in the business of promoting people who didn't contribute to the bottom line. Ebby was helping Miss O'Shea's operation perform in difficult times. Well-run companies like Consolidated Millinery identified, developed, and promoted promising employees. Not only was it the right thing to do, it also made good business sense. Miss O'Shea recommended Ebby to manage Consolidated's new location in Omaha, Nebraska.

If she accepted, Ebby would move out of the basement and on to the first floor of the Herzberg Department Store where Consolidated leased space. She would also get another jump in salary to $125 per month. Ebby had her misgivings. The move would take her two hundred miles farther from Junction City, Kansas, where her mother, Lucille, and her sister, Franky, and brother, Paul, now lived. Ebby had not seen her family in months, and the move would make visits more difficult. She was concerned that Omaha was smaller than Kansas City, half its size. She wondered if she could sell enough hats to earn her salary. She also had doubts about the Nebraska economy. A drought was scorching the Great Plains and decimating large sections of farm land. A move to Omaha also meant icy cold winters. She had lived in cold weather before, but Omaha in December would be arctic compared to anything she had experienced.

Ebby thought about her option overnight and in the morning told Miss O'Shea she would take the job. She was bound for a position she had never held, in a city she had never seen, without friends, and in a country ruined by unemployment, poverty, homelessness, and farm losses. Ebby recognized the challenges and confidently stepped aboard the train—business as usual for the intrepid twenty-four-year-old.

## WORKING THE ROOM

Assessing the difficulties ahead and plunging forward was a skill Ebby honed over many years. In 1957, after more than four years crossing the country, bad meals, lumpy beds, and speaking in a wide range of venues, Ebby knew how to play to her audience. Each of her speeches had to accomplish four things: express a clear point of view, speak directly to the audience, give solid information, and get to the point. This last objective— getting to the point—was possibly more important than all the others combined. The last thing business people wanted was a luncheon or dinner speaker who couldn't finish talking before they finished eating. Ebby's speaking success was in her delivery and her message, not in how long she took to say it.

Late that year, Ebby spoke at the University of Michigan School of Business at its annual two-day real estate symposium. She was the only woman on the program. Next, she flew to Baton Rouge, Louisiana, and appeared with the dean of the Louisiana State University College of Commerce and the president of the Louisiana Board of Realtors at a real estate round table. The event was open to anyone interested in real estate as a career. Each member of the panel said a few words, and then the group fielded questions for the remainder of the evening. Later she was asked why she bothered attending at all, why take a nine-hundred-mile trip to answer a few questions from people who may never work in real estate?

"Because," Ebby said, "the event was close to the Louisiana State University campus. I thought there might be a few young people in the audience. And if there were, I wanted them to consider a career in real estate. I wanted them to know what was involved, how to get started, and some of the benefits."

Two weeks later, she spoke in Mission, a suburb of Kansas City, Kansas. Later, she gave presentations in and around Dallas in May and June, and in Beaumont, Texas, in July. Beaumont had become one of her favorite stops. This was her third visit in four years. The *Beaumont Journal* predicted a standing-room-only audience for Ebby's luncheon talk on "The Atomic Age Businesswomen."

Later, an editor for the Lion's Club newsletter described her as a Dallasite of many achievements, cool as an autumn morning, crisp as sugar-cured breakfast bacon, and warm and sweet as pancakes and syrup. According to the editor, Ebby's talk was spiced with rib-tickling humor, contained a handful of interesting facts, and took less than a quarter hour. The local press also praised her for getting to the point. A follow-up news article told readers that Ebby had a secret—not her broad smile, her winning personality, or that she had something to say. Her secret was in saying it and sitting down.

# CHAPTER FIVE
## From Stranger to Partner:
## Waiting Can Be a Good Thing

At the conclusion of the Beaumont event, a bellman at the hotel escorted Ebby to a courtesy car waiting to shuttle guests to the airport. In the front passenger seat sat a well-dressed man engrossed in his newspaper. Ebby climbed into the backseat behind the driver. As the car pulled away, the man folded his newspaper and absently placed it on the seat between himself and the driver. He turned to the driver, "It says here that Castro is still holding thirty of our Marines down there in Cuba."

Ebby spoke up, "Batista had better figure out a way to get that guy to surrender. Otherwise we're going to have socialism ninety miles from Florida."

The passenger rotated in his seat and nodded at Ebby. "Maurice Acers," he said. "It's spelled A-C-E-R-S, but rhymes with bakers."

"Ebby Halliday."

"Ebby," he said.

"That's right."

"Let me ask you. Do you think President Eisenhower is tolerating Castro or provoking him?"

"I don't think it makes any difference. If Castro takes hold of Cuba, we'll have no choice but to recognize the new government."

The two continued talking on the ride to the airport, mostly about politics—the upcoming Democratic presidential nominee and Texas politics. Toward the end of the ride, Maurice Acers asked what Ebby thought of the space race and Sputnik. They ran out of time before they ran out of topics. In the Beaumont airport, they said their goodbyes.

Maurice turned to go, but stopped. "Perhaps we could resume this conversation sometime when I am passing through Dallas."

"I would be delighted," Ebby said. She handed him a business card.

He handed her a card of his own and pointed at his last name. "Acers, rhymes with bakers."

"I won't forget."

So began a relationship that would last the rest of their lives together.

# IDENTIFYING COMMON GROUND

Maurice Wilson Acers and Ebby Halliday had a lot in common. Both were born into working-class families. Both grew up in the Midwest. Both fought hard to find their place in the world. And both would become uncommonly successful in their chosen fields. Maurice was born in 1907 in Dallas, Texas. His father, Ed Acers, was the founder of Acers Wood, Coal, Feed, Fuel, and Ice Company, a small outfit that delivered goods to homeowners and businesses using teams of horse-drawn wagons. When Ed would allow, Maurice helped drive the wagon on deliveries.

When Maurice was fourteen, he enrolled in the Reserve Officers Training Corps and later graduated near the top of his high school class. With good grades, he had his choice of universities. Out of love and respect for his mother, Effie, Maurice elected to stay in Dallas and attend Southern Methodist University, a private university that was, in effect, the official college of the Methodist Church west of the Mississippi. The university was relatively new, having opened its doors only ten years earlier. A chapter of the Phi Delta Theta had already been established, and the fraternity extended an invitation to the freshman Dallasite to join. Maurice graduated from SMU in the spring of 1929 and immediately got accepted to Harvard Law School.

Being admitted to Harvard was one thing; paying for it was another. To earn his way, Maurice worked as many hours as he could. He lived at home and saved nearly all his earnings. By the fall, Maurice was sure he had enough money for tuition and books, at least enough for the first semester. Harvard University was half a country away, and the trip to Cambridge, Massachusetts, was an arduous eighteen-hundred-mile, three-day train ride. When he arrived, he had two priorities: get to know his way around and find a job.

In the 1920s and 1930s, Cambridge was one of the main industrial cities of New England, with nearly one hundred and twenty thousand residents. Maurice took a stroll through the campus, Harvard Yard, and the triangular Harvard Square. He watched lazy canoers paddling the Charles River. He sat in the shade taking in one of Cambridge's well-known landmarks, the imposing Weld Boathouse, base for Harvard's rowing and crew teams.

His next chore, finding a job, would prove more difficult. Coinciding with Maurice's arrival in Cambridge, the American stock market and the Dow Jones Industrial Average hit an all-time high of 381 in September 1929. Soon after, everything changed. The market lost 17 percent of its value the following month. On October 29, in a single day, the stock market lost an unprecedented $14 billion in value. The day was later christened "Black Tuesday." Whether the market crash caused the Great Depression or simply coincided with the worldwide economic downtown of the Roaring Twenties didn't matter to most people, including Maurice. The result was the same—bankruptcies, business closures, and soaring unemployment.

Given the state of the economy, Maurice could not find a job. No job meant no tuition money for next semester. No tuition meant no Harvard Law. To make matters worse, Harvard's scholarship portfolio was in shambles. Any hope of financial assistance from the university was wishful thinking. Having already paid for his first semester, Maurice started classes and dove headlong into his studies. The first-year law curriculum was punishing—constitutional law, civil procedure, torts, property, and contracts.

The reading and casework required all his concentration. Anything that diluted that concentration had to be pushed aside or buried altogether. Yet try as he might, he couldn't stop thinking about money. How would he pay for next semester? How would he cover his rent and food in the coming months?

Law students at the university fell into two camps: those who could afford to continue next semester and those who could not. And if he couldn't afford to continue, the thinking went, why bother to read and study and prepare for final exams that he might never sit for. Exams weren't until January, and many members of the entering class already knew they wouldn't make it until then. By the time Christmas arrived, he had made up his mind. Maurice would not return for first semester finals. Returning to Dallas would give him time to rethink his future. Despite the hardships and the inauspicious start, he wasn't despondent. On the contrary, he had learned a valuable lesson: In any situation, there are things you can control and things you can't. The challenge is to know the difference and make decisions accordingly.

## DIGGING IN

Maurice Acers understood that he couldn't control the economy. He couldn't control the stock market or the rate of unemployment. He couldn't control the price of tuition or rent or food. He could control his own thoughts, his own choices, and his own actions. Returning to Dallas was the right decision. In 1930, Dallasites were doing better than most. Oil speculators had recently struck oil east of Dallas prompting the East Texas oil boom. Oil workers and roustabouts willing to put in long hours under grueling conditions could find work. For Dallas city dwellers, things weren't so hopeful. Prices climbed and wages fell. Auto sales declined. In farming areas, commodity prices plunged.

Maurice immediately began working at several part-time jobs. He worked during the day and planned his future at night. He wasn't ready to give up on law school. Many universities would accept him, but the most logical choice was the University of Texas at Austin, a short two hundred miles south. The UT School of Law had a good reputation, and the tuition was affordable. He would still need to work to put himself through school, but with the reduced tuition, he just might make enough.

Austin was a college town and a state capital but not much else. In the 1930s, the city didn't have a viable commercial or industrial base and had a population of only fifty-three thousand. Austin also didn't have a lot of part-time jobs for twenty-three-year-old law students. The largest employers were the university and the government. City, county, and state government agencies posted a handful of job openings. The problem was that they had little interest in hiring students. Employers willing to take on part-time help had their pick of the bunch. Job-seeking students were as plentiful as Texas oak trees.

Maurice dug in, redoubled his efforts, and landed not one, but two jobs—a sales position in a men's clothing store and a second job as janitor at a department store. The sales job paid a small hourly salary and a commission on sales. The cleaning job didn't pay much, but it required only three hours of work each evening after the store closed. Law school and two jobs made for an ambitious schedule. It left little time for anything else. Maurice was determined to make a go of it, and he knew with a little organization and a lot of discipline, he could make it all work.

By the end of the first semester, Maurice's formula for study and work proved successful. His grades put him in the top quarter of his class. The following semester was harder. The course material was all new. The lecturers were new. Even the students in class and his study groups were all new. He organized. He planned each day's activities. He minimized social commitments and kept the same rigorous work schedule rather than quit one or both of his jobs. It would be easier to quit work, no doubt, but if he left a job, there was no guarantee of finding another when he needed it. In hindsight, he made the right decision. His grades slipped, but not enough to matter.

With the summer approaching, Maurice had to decide whether to return to Dallas or remain in Austin. He opted to stay in Austin and forego three months of free room and board. Leaving now meant starting the job search all over again when he returned in September. Throughout the summer, he picked up additional jobs, mowing lawns and cleaning flower beds. Maintaining a natty lawn was a luxury in the 1930s, and only a handful of homeowners had the spare cash. By the end of the summer, the job market grew tight. Worse, the price of labor dropped to pennies an hour. By the time returning students flooded back to the UT campus in 1931, Maurice had enough cash tucked away to pay for tuition and books for the coming semester.

The second year law curriculum was even more demanding—taxation, federal courts, business associations, and criminal law. In addition to the mountains of reading and writing required by law school, Maurice held onto his jobs throughout the year. By the end of 1932, thousands of city, county, and state workers were laid off, many of whom now turned to federal relief programs like the Civilian Conservation Corps. The CCC put young men to work outdoors and gave old people a small income so they had money for things they needed. The city of Austin sponsored plays and musicals, the proceeds of which went to support charities. Churches and private charities opened breadlines and soup kitchens, which served up watery soup, to feed hungry residents. Later, the county took over and opened shelters for hundreds and later thousands of needy people.

Nearly a quarter of the population was unemployed. What ensued was economic panic. Americans stopped spending. Businesses closed. Defaulted loans sent banks into a tailspin, wiping out bank reserves along with depositors' savings. Widespread bank failures caused other depositors to make a run on surviving banks, jeopardizing the stability of the entire banking industry. By the end of the 1930s, more than nine thousand banks had closed, swallowing up more than $140 billion in depositor savings. Faced with this mountain of economic uncertainty, Maurice had a choice. He could continue with his exhausting schedule and hope his jobs didn't vanish, or he could take a temporary one-year position with a new federal agency.

## STEPPING BACKWARD TO MARCH FORWARD

President Herbert Hoover had a plan to combat the Depression. He called it the Reconstruction Finance Corporation. With the new agency, Hoover planned to give $2 billion in aid to state and local governments and make loans to banks, railroads, and farm mortgage associations. An Austin office of the RFC was scheduled to open in the fall of 1932, and one of Maurice's customers from the clothing store had been tapped to manage the agency's Austin location. Knowing Maurice's work ethic and educational background, and surmising a bit about his finances, the customer asked Maurice if he was interested in putting his degree on hold for a year. The agency needed an analyst. The pay was astoundingly high. Completing his law degree was important, but even if he finished school on time, no one was hiring. It was an easy decision. Maurice went to work for the Reconstruction Finance Corporation.

The RFC made short-term loans to banks hoping the loans would help banks survive any run on deposits. Early in the agency's history, Congress threw a wrench into the works. The U.S. Congress implemented regulations that required all banks borrowing from the RFC to disclose the bank's name. A bank advertising that it borrowed money was all but hanging a big sign on the front door that read, "Bank on shaky ground." RFC's goal was to build consumer confidence and prevent a run on banks, whereas disclosing the bank's own borrowing practices had the opposite effect: it scared depositors away. In the end, the RFC's loan programs failed to stem the tide of failing banks.

In 1932, the newly elected President Franklin Delano Roosevelt had other plans for the RFC. The agency could be used to finance a variety of projects without obtaining legislative approval. Far from seeing his job eliminated by the change of administrations, Maurice inadvertently found himself employed by one of the prominent New Deal agencies. Maurice figured that the new administration's plan for the agency would give him an extra six months of employment before he returned to school in the fall.

While Maurice was looking to complete his last year of law school, the nation had become both awed and enamored by a new wave of criminals, what Frank Loesch of the Chicago Crime Commission called "public enemies." Al Capone, John Dillinger, Charles "Pretty Boy" Floyd, Lester "Baby Face" Nelson, Kate "Ma" Barker, and others had captured the imagination of millions of Americans. Many of the criminals were larger than life. Flamboyant bootlegger Al Capone, for example, was smart. He was brutal. And he was organized. If the government couldn't handle the country's economic problems, how then could it hope to deal with organized crime? Al Capone and others like him were only part of the problem. The media helped turn these criminals into romantic figures. The bank robber, John Dillinger, was idolized when newspapers throughout the Midwest reported that in a recent bank robbery he had destroyed mortgage and loan records in an effort to help the little guy who faced foreclosure or loan default.

Often the news of organized crimes was shocking. In 1933, for instance, four special agents and three police officers were transporting bank robber Frank "Jelly" Nash from Kansas City's Union Station to the federal penitentiary at Leavenworth, Kansas. After Nash was loaded into a car, three men carrying machine guns fired into the car, killing three police officers, one agent, and Nash, whom they had hoped to free. The Kansas City Massacre, as it was called, riveted the nation. Newspapers, movie newsreels, and radio kept the story alive for months, with almost daily details of the search for the killers. One of the shooters, Vernon Miller, surfaced four months later, beaten to death. Two other shooters, Adam Richelli and "Pretty Boy" Floyd, eluded authorities for months.

More than a year later, Floyd was spotted in Ohio and killed in a shootout with local police. Richetti was captured in the same incident, placed on trial for murder, and executed four years later.

At about the same time Maurice Acers was reading about the Kansas City Massacre, Ebby Halliday, four years his junior, was busy at work at The Jones Store in Kansas City. On a Saturday in June, she heard police and ambulance sirens screaming through the busy streets. Not twelve blocks away, the Kansas City Massacre was going down just outside Union Station. Floyd, Miller, and Richetti were blanketing a car with bullets, trying to free "Jelly" Nash.

The entire city was transformed in a matter of seconds. Even in the basement of The Jones Store, Ebby could hear and feel the panic outside. The Kansas City grapevine was fast. Minutes after the shootout, shoppers were spreading the word: several people had been shot at Union Station. A special edition of the *Kansas City Star* reported the story a few hours later: Well-armed gangsters had tried to free their bank-robbing pal. A hundred and twenty miles away in Junction City, Ebby's mother, Lucille, read the same story and immediately wrote her daughter, suggesting she cancel her planned trip home. Ebby should stay off the streets, she pleaded, where it wasn't safe. Prohibition and bootleggers had led to widespread disrespect for the law, and Lucille had genuine concerns about her daughter's safety.

The Kansas City Massacre was a turning point for Maurice Acers. He developed an awareness of evil in the world, an understanding that crime in America was organizing and gangs were turning into criminal organizations. The sheer volume of crime stories in the newspapers and in newsreels had become numbing. In a recent story, a special commission of the Texas Highway Patrol had finally caught up with notorious bank robbers and murderers, Bonnie Parker and Clyde Barrow. It had taken authorities two years and a dozen deaths, nine of which were law enforcement officers, to pigeonhole the two near their northern Louisiana hideout. Parker and Barrow were shot and killed by a posse of four Texas and two Louisiana officers. The date, May 23, 1934, was within days of Maurice's graduation from law school.

The fight against America's public enemies had captured Maurice's attention. After graduation, Maurice Wilson Acers joined the United States Bureau of Investigation, later known as the Federal Bureau of Investigation.

## BEFRIENDING STRANGERS

There was something fearless about Maurice Acers, and Ebby sensed it from that first chance encounter in Beaumont, Texas. Befriending strangers was second nature to Ebby. Perhaps that explained her instant attraction. Because of her prominence in real estate, Ebby usually made the invitations. With Maurice, she found the situation refreshing, a new acquaintance unaware of her local celebrity. In hindsight, real estate had never come up in conversation, a first for Ebby. The conversation was lively, but what she liked most of all was the confident resonance of his voice.

Ebby had an exhausting schedule, and as much as she might like to spend more time with Maurice Acers, he would have to wait. After Beaumont, she spoke in Austin at the Texas Real Estate Association about the opportunities in real estate available to women, especially women over forty. "In fact," she said, "a mature woman has an advantage over a younger woman. A real estate transaction is a big piece of business. The client must respect the woman's ability to handle the financial part of the transaction. I think a mature woman has a better chance of commanding such respect." She advised women to get training. Enroll in their local colleges and universities. Learn the financial, ethical, legal, and business sides of the industry.

In September 1958, Ebby was the breakfast speaker for the opening session of the New Mexico Real Estate Board's annual real estate school. If the title of her speech, "Ten Million Dollar Selling," wasn't sufficient to arouse the audience's enthusiasm, her torpedo-style delivery certainly was. Ebby enthusiastically aimed her words at her audience and let loose her native optimism in well-timed blasts. Her spirit set the tone for the two-day meeting. She recounted her thirteen-year history in real estate and how she had gotten her start with the insulated cement houses.

Two weeks later, she spoke at the Ohio Real Estate Boards annual convention with more than twelve thousand agents in attendance. Three days later, she addressed the Minnesota Association of Realtors; then she was on to Oklahoma City where she spoke at the Oklahoma Association of Realtors' annual convention. A newspaper columnist described her this way: "She's Ebby Halliday, and she's been gadding about the country selling an idea—the real estate business is a woman's world. Sounds easy. It isn't." Ebby was never confrontational when she spoke about women in real estate. She believed what she said and made her case as plainly as possible. The real estate industry needed more women, especially in key positions, such as the boardroom. She told convention goers that women were natural leaders. They could handle the tough jobs. She also said the situation would likely right itself soon enough. The role of women in real estate was evolving on its own, but it was also her mission to encourage women to stand up and get involved.

A week later, Ebby spoke in Seattle to the Washington Association of Realtors at their annual educational conference. Then she flew north for a quick visit to Anchorage, accepting a personal invitation from the only female director of the Anchorage Chamber of Commerce to the only female director of the North Dallas Chamber of Commerce to talk about ways to encourage more women to choose real estate as a career. Returning to Dallas, she prepared for two presentations in San Francisco, California, at the upcoming annual convention of the National Association of Real Estate Boards. The NAREB convention was held in a different city each year: New York in 1955, St. Louis in 1956, Detroit in 1957, and now San Francisco in 1958. At the conclusion of the convention, the chairman announced the 1959 convention location would be Toronto, Canada. Toronto was a startling choice, and it got Ebby thinking. If Toronto could host the industry's largest convention next year, why not Dallas in 1960?

As busy as she was, running a rapidly-expanding company, chairing committees, staying in touch with colleagues, and keeping a ferocious public speaking schedule, Ebby still had moments to herself. In those moments, she thought about Maurice Acers, about the confidence in his manner, about his voice and the way he introduced himself: "Acers. Rhymes with bakers," unpretentiously in a Texas drawl she found charming. Maurice had called the number on her business card, her office number, several times, but each time she was gadding about the country as the Oklahoma columnist so accurately described. Her career, and especially her speaking career, had taken on a life of its own, one that left little time for personal relationships.

## STAYING IN TOUCH

Back in Dallas, Ebby discovered that Maurice Acers had called again. This time he left a message saying he would be in Dallas during the holidays. He hoped they could have dinner when he was in town. Unfortunately, she was already booked for the holidays. She had a business trip planned to the island nation of Granada off the coast of South America, where clients were considering an investment opportunity. She wrote Maurice a short letter expressing her regret and explained the circumstances. She closed by mentioning that her travel schedule was jam-packed for months. She didn't expect to see daylight until the middle of next year. Most men would have been put off by such a lengthy delay. Most men would have taken this short missive as a polite sign to go away. Maurice Acers, it turned out, wasn't most men.

Her letter was not, in fact, a coded message to stop calling. It was the truth jotted down in Ebby's straightforward style. And she meant what she said. Her calendar was chock-full of engagements, beginning in 1959 with her speaking at the Dayton Real Estate Board. She gave a rousing forecast of the real estate market based on what she perceived as positive population growth, a rise in personal income, and an increasingly mobile workforce.

This was the first public speech in which she also chided the government for its manipulation of the federal housing administration and veterans' administration programs. She told the audience that the government was attempting to stabilize an overheated housing market by limiting the number of housing starts, a bad idea, in Ebby's opinion. She firmly believed that the government had no business using housing programs as economic tools. To make her case, she gave the following humorous example: "Socialism is when you have two cows and you share the milk with everyone else. Communism is when you have two cows; the government takes the cows and gives you the milk. Fascism is when you have two cows; the government takes the cows and sells you the milk. Nazism is when you have two cows; the government takes the cows and shoots you. Capitalism is when you have two cows; you sell one—and buy a bull."

She returned to Dallas, tweaked her Dayton speech, which she renamed "Selling in Orbit," and spoke at several Dallas-area real estate clubs. Weeks later, she gave a talk at the Indianapolis Real Estate Board. A reporter from the *Indianapolis Times* called her a charmer who flattered a throng of professionals by describing how to be even more successful in real estate. She told attendees to concentrate on private enterprise as an approach to urban renewal. She emphasized a Realtor's role in the community. And she reminded the Realtors of their responsibility to be advocates of progress.

Three weeks later, she was the featured speaker at the Alberta Real Estate Association annual convention, where she gave this advice: "At Ebby Halliday Realtors, we expect women to act like ladies and do business like men." In her office that meant all female agents were required to wear tailored clothes, tasteful jewelry, and simple hats. Ebby never shied away from giving practical advice. She said, "Women in business must be emotionally stable. They should forget about ego. Most of all, never take advantage of your femininity." Her advice to women didn't stop there. Women in real estate should like people, like houses, be able to organize their time, and recognize that real estate is a full-time job. She said they must be willing to give up evenings and weekends, gain insight to their profession, and take advantage of every opportunity to further that knowledge. She said, "We want women who have well-organized households. We don't want an agent to break off in the middle of signing a contract to phone home and ask about Junior." She reminded Alberta convention goers that the first impression they made was all-important. Clients respected a person of good taste. They respected agents who set gossip aside and shared factual, verifiable, and relevant information.

In the past two years, she had traveled to every state in the nation. She had plans to visit Hawaii as soon as it became the fiftieth state later that year. Friends told her all the travel would make an old woman of her. "What if it does make an old woman out of me?" she told a reporter. "Think of the wonderful memories I'll have."

Ebby had an excellent memory. She remembered exactly the last time she had spoken to Maurice Acers. It was six months ago. And in those six months, she hadn't heard a peep out of him. In hindsight, it was probably her own fault. She was the one who said she'd be busy for the first half of the year. Was that really any reason not to call? Men, and especially men like Maurice, she realized only now, could be *too* logical sometimes. They could take a woman too literally. In not calling for all these months, Maurice had given her a clue to his personality, his thinking process, and his values. He valued words, for example. When Ebby said she would be busy for the first half of the year, Maurice took it to mean six months.

In June, Maurice called, six months to the day since his last call. On the phone, he noted the surprise in her voice and told her he'd put her number in his calendar. "You said June, and here it is June. I called. What is there to be surprised about?" He would be in Dallas in August on a business matter. He asked if she might join him for dinner one evening. "Certainly," Ebby told him. He was exacting and meticulous, she thought, but he was also a patient man. He was way more patient than Ebby, in fact. She had waited this long. She could wait a little longer.

# CHAPTER SIX
## Taking Risks

In August, Maurice Acers called again. He let Ebby select the date and time for their upcoming dinner meeting, and he selected the restaurant. Two weeks later, Ebby found herself getting ready for an evening out with a man she had met for all of thirty minutes a year earlier. In truth, she knew very little about Maurice Acers. He was persistent. He was punctual. He had a woodsy deep telephone voice. That was about it.

By chance, Maurice had selected one of Ebby's favorite restaurants. The place was a small, out-of-the-way bistro where she frequently took clients to celebrate a sale. Maurice arrived early. He watched Ebby drive up in her black Cadillac and hand the keys to a valet.

Inside, the maître d' looked confused. Ebby was a regular, and she understood the situation right away.

"The reservation is under Acers," she said.

"Yes, yes. I see it here."

Before the meal arrived, the two made small talk. Ebby asked about Maurice's visit to Dallas.

"An investment," he said. "I'm always looking for good investments."

"Property, you mean?"

"Mostly, yes."

Ebby talked about her recent trip to Granada, the beaches, the white sand, and the smell of cinnamon and clove wherever she went. She represented clients looking for a second home, something on the beach.

"Sound's a bit exotic for me," Maurice said. "I would be interested in hearing more about other investments. Something closer to home perhaps."

"So this is a working dinner?"

"Not at all. In fact, if you don't mind, let me tell you a bit about myself."

He told Ebby about his father's small business, how the warehouse had been located less than a mile from where they sat that evening. He talked about growing up and about college and gave a short version of his current duties as a commissioner of the Texas Employment Commission. But what Ebby liked most were stories about Maurice's years in the FBI. Ebby understood that great rewards often came at great risk—opening a business, investing in real estate, or the critical decision-making it took to advance a career. All these opportunities contained within them a high degree of risk, and Ebby thrived on understanding and challenging those risks.

## FACING DOWN THE MENACE

Maurice Acers was no stranger to risk. His years at the FBI had been anything but peril free. By 1934, when Maurice first entered the Federal Bureau of Investigations, the agency had been molded in the image of its controversial director, J. Edgar Hoover. When Hoover had taken over ten years earlier, he had immediately fired unqualified agents, abolished seniority as the main criterion for promotions, introduced uniform performance appraisals, and established a formal training program for new agents.

Maurice began his training in Washington, D.C.; it consisted primarily of lectures and rigorous tests about investigative methods and evidence. Hoover wanted to outsmart criminals rather than outmuscle them and therefore preferred special agents with law or accounting degrees. The bureau placed an almost fanatical emphasis on legal issues and audit procedures. Missing from the curriculum was training in firearms because, at the time, agents did not carry weapons. Little wonder that the public felt federal law enforcement was no match for organized crime. Lawyers and accountants armed with briefcases and adding machines were no match for organized thugs with submachine guns. This policy would soon change, however, in response to the ongoing crime wave.

After his training, Maurice was sent to the San Francisco office and assigned to a recent kidnapping case. On May 24, 1935, nine-year-old George Weyerhaeuser, son of wealthy lumberman J.P. Weyerhaeuser, was abducted in Tacoma, Washington. A ransom note demanded two hundred thousand dollars. After gathering the money, the FBI recorded the serial numbers of the bills. During the ransom drop, agents lost sight of J.P. Weyerhaeuser, but good to their word, the kidnappers released young George unharmed two days later. Within a few days, a woman was apprehended passing the recorded bills at a five-and-ten-cent store near Salt Lake City. She later admitted that her husband and an accomplice had masterminded the Weyerhaeuser kidnapping. The woman's husband, Harmon Waley, was quickly caught, convicted, and sentenced to forty-five years at the federal prison on Alcatraz Island in San Francisco Bay. Margaret Waley was sentenced to twenty years in the United States Detention Farm in Milan, Michigan.

Special Agent Maurice Acers's task was to track down Waley's accomplice, one William Dainard. Maurice interviewed Waley at Alcatraz Federal Prison and created a profile of personality and behavioral characteristics, which he hoped would lead him to Dainard. The process was slow and arduous and required many trips to the prison. After months of effort, Agent Acers's hard work led to naught because Dainard all but stumbled into the FBI's lap.

In 1936, the Los Angeles office of the FBI notified other west coast offices that a man fitting Dainard's description was exchanging some of the stolen twenty-dollar bills at banks in LA. They also passed along a possible license plate number. On a hunch, the San Francisco Special Agent in Charge guessed that Dainard might be moving north and assigned agents to stake out local banks.

After the briefing, an agent noticed a car across the street from the FBI building with the hood up and a man staring at the motor. On instinct, the agent checked the license plate, and it was a match.

FBI agents came in all shapes and sizes. At least they did until Director Hoover took over. In addition to imposing an age requirement for beginning agents, he also created a minimum height criterion of five feet eight inches. Maurice had thought to himself on occasion that a particular agent in the office must have been wearing elevated heels the day of his physical examination. But at this particular moment, five-feet-whatever would be more than enough to get the job done.

Approaching the suspect directly from behind, the agent noticed that the man was now leaning over the fender and working on something inside the engine compartment. He also noted that the suspect was not wearing a coat on the chilly morning. Under these conditions and from this angle, there was one obvious solution. The agent produced his newly issued revolver from its holster, shoved the business end into the protruding body part, and said in his best G-Man voice, "Don't move a muscle, or I'll blow your brains out from back here." Mr. Smith and Mr. Wesson could not have been more proud.

Two days later, William Dainard pleaded guilty and was sentenced to sixty years in the U.S. Penitentiary at Leavenworth, Kansas. Dainard was later confined to the prison hospital for the criminally insane.

Ebby loved the story. It had all the elements of good drama: risk, conflict, and a fair amount of justice. She had her own stories to share, nothing quite so daring, but they had been daring enough for a young girl in a new city all by herself.

## CAPITALIZING ON CHANCE

In late 1934, around the time Maurice was meeting with Harmon Waley in the dank cells of Alcatraz Prison, Ebby had been on her way to Omaha, Nebraska, to manage a new store location for Consolidated Millinery. She was taking a chance on the new position, a chance that unemployment, poverty, homelessness, and farm losses would not prevent her from making a go of it. She was taking a chance that at twenty-four she could be successful on her own.

As soon as she stepped off the train, she gave her new surroundings a sympathetic gaze. A brutal drought had scorched the Nebraska countryside, drying up the soil and withering the endless miles of cornfields. Omaha was at the northeastern tip of the Dust Bowl, what some called the "Dirty Thirties," a hundred million acres of baked, lifeless topsoil and dust storms, centered on the panhandles of Texas and Oklahoma and the states of New Mexico, Colorado, and Kansas. At times, the sky blackened and a heartless wind scooped up the loose earth, carried it overhead, and dumped it into the Atlantic Ocean a thousand miles away. Jackrabbits were blown into fences and smothered by one another when they were unable to escape.

At the Omaha train station, crowds milled about, waiting to board outbound trains. Other people strained to catch sight of disembarking passengers. What made Ebby smile was how well-dressed every one was. Nearly every woman wore a hat.

Money was tight, but hats were a fashion statement that refused to die without a fight. For the last couple of decades, women, and men, just didn't feel dressed without a hat. During the Depression, not as many hats were sold. People wore the hats they had. Old and well worn as their hats might be, many people put off a new purchase until the time was right. But eventually everything wears out, or the color fades, or the style changes. When women were ready for a new hat, Ebby would be there to make the sale. By the time she stepped from the train, she had all the understanding and confidence she needed to believe she could be successful in her new town.

Within days of her arrival, Ebby learned quickly what Omahans most valued. She could sum it up in one word—football. The University of Nebraska, only sixty miles southwest in Lincoln, had one of the best college football teams in the nation. The previous year, the team finished with a stellar record—eight wins and one loss. Throughout the Midwest, the University of Nebraska team was known as the Cornhuskers, or just the Huskers, and with D.X. Bible as head coach, the game was revered as part religion and part sport. Football, Ebby came to realize, was even more important in difficult times. Fans wanted heroes who reflected their ethics and values, heroes who could go head-to-head with adversity and win. Coach Bible did just that. He delivered six Big Six Conference championships in eight years at Nebraska before leaving for the University of Texas in 1937.

Ebby soon assimilated into the Nebraska culture. If her customers were talking football, so was she. More than a few of her customers at the Herzberg department store were football fans. She was constantly improving her sales techniques, and that meant understanding your customers, whatever their preferences. Along with updating her football vocabulary, she learned to hone her insight into company overhead, inventory management, and profit margins. Ebby was the manager now, and that meant selling, but it also meant ensuring that Consolidated Millinery's Omaha location contributed to the company's bottom line.

Consolidated's sales department was on the first floor of the Herzberg store, a prime selling location. For women who had the means, hats were inexpensive enough to buy on impulse. While a woman might think twice about buying a new dress, a hat was a mere accessory. A hat was far from a major purchase. On the contrary, she told her customers, a hat was an ornament that contributed to the overall style of the outfit. Choose the right hat, and add the panache needed to turn simple into spectacular. Of course, being on the main floor meant more customer traffic and more impulse purchases.

The main floor had high ceilings and wide windows. Ebby's location got lots of light and sunshine throughout the day, a boost to her naturally good mood. Ebby was a natural salesperson. She had the personality, the looks, and the ability to engage people. She also had a good memory. She remembered faces, and she remembered names. Mrs. Henningson, for instance, and her eighteen-year-old daughter, Margre, visited the hat department regularly. Ebby and Mrs. Henningson hit it off, so much so that as Mrs. Henningson was trying on a classic Peachbloom Velour hat in a moving cobalt blue, she confided that her youngest daughter had died years earlier, a mix up with a prescription. That Ms. Henningson confided in her affected Ebby deeply. She loved selling, but she equally loved those rare occasions when she connected with people on a personal level.

Ebby's hat sales improved year after year. Three years into her new life in Omaha, she had a steady flow of repeat business. Omaha was growing. The local economy was improving. In June

1938, a Consolidated Millinery regional sales manager arrived in Omaha. The manager made regular rounds, meeting with the department store management in an effort to maintain good relations and sitting down with individual Consolidated store managers like Ebby. During his talk with Ebby, he confessed that he was surprised that Consolidated's Omaha location was doing so well. Sales continued to grow, ties between the department store and Ebby were strong, and the future looked impressive, if not predictable. The manager, a slight man with an unusually thin mustache, had only one question.

"We have an opening for a manager. It's a key position in one of our top locations. What do you say?"

"What exactly are you asking me?"

"Yes, of course, I'm being vague. Would you consider a move to Dallas?"

"Dallas, Texas. That Dallas?"

"Our manager at the W.A. Green Department Store is retiring. Based on what you've done here, I think you would be a perfect fit."

"Dallas," she said again.

"The move, if you agree, comes with a raise." He reached for his briefcase and pulled out a small file. He glanced at a page and then closed the file. "I believe that would take you to $175 a month."

"You're offering me a larger store, more money, and a climate without snow. Am I leaving anything out?"

The manager smiled, pushed his chair back, and reached for his briefcase. The impression was that the deal was done.

"How long do I have to think about it?" Ebby asked.

# TRADING CERTAINTY FOR PROMOTION

About the same time Ebby contemplated her next move, Maurice had a similar decision to make. Shortly after the Weyerhaeuser kidnapping case, the San Francisco Special Agent in Charge recommended Maurice for a promotion. At the FBI, however, offer and acceptance were ceremonial—rarely did an agent decline a promotion. The advance meant a move to Washington, D.C., for additional training. This was one of many transfers throughout Maurice's career to cities like Pittsburgh, Dallas, Oklahoma City, and Detroit, including a stint in London at Scotland Yard. In 1938, Maurice was chosen as the first official exchange student between the FBI and Scotland Yard. His task was to study the history of Scotland Yard from an American perspective. His report was subsequently published in a limited edition book titled *The Police of England*.

As a result of ongoing favorable reviews, Maurice continued to move through the FBI ranks. By the spring of 1941, he was in line for appointment as the Special Agent in Charge of the San Antonio office, which was the second oldest field office in the Bureau behind only New York. At one time, it covered the entire territory west of the Mississippi River. Running the office was a distinguished position, and it meant a return to his home state.

Special Agent in Charge Maurice Acers took the position. When he arrived in San Antonio in the early 1940s, unemployment was around 14 percent, and the crime rate was equally high, he told Ebby. But that was a story for another day.

Maurice sipped his coffee and took a small bite of his crème brulee. He offered Ebby a bite. She waved the dessert away.

"Tell me more about the Bureau," she said.

"You, first. Did you take the job in Dallas? My guess is you did, or we wouldn't be sitting here having a dinner as nice as this."

"That, too, I'll save for another time."

She talked briefly about her busy speaking schedule, how she believed it was helping to build her business. He was fascinated that a girl born in the hills of Arkansas had grown into the woman before him. They talked football, fashion, food, and movies until the coffee was gone and the small bistro was vacant. They agreed to do it again sometime, perhaps the next time Maurice was traveling through Dallas, perhaps when Ebby was in Austin. Until then, they had more than enough to think about.

# CHAPTER SEVEN
## Growing with Dallas

Dinner with Maurice was a rare moment of calm, but it didn't last. The following morning, Ebby composed a short note to Maurice and dropped it in the mail; otherwise, she had little time to ponder her feelings. With no out-of-town speeches scheduled for late 1958, she had her plate full, catching up on business. Traveling as much as she did meant delegating decisions to others. Now was the time to take the pulse of her organization. She had a list of key areas to review: sales training, agent staffing, marketing, accounting, space requirements, and administrative support.

To help her stay on track, Ebby hired a young assistant, Mary Frances Burleson. She was a sophomore at Southern Methodist University, and she needed the job to help pay for tuition. The twenty-three-year-old signed up with a temporary employment agency that sent her to interview with Ebby Halliday Realtors. The interview went well, and Mary Frances got the job. It paid $2.50 an hour; Mary Frances was glad to have it.

Initially, she worked part time in the afternoons, taking messages and typing correspondence. In between her regular duties, Mary Frances found ways to streamline some of the administrative functions by identifying problem areas, getting rid of the clutter, and creating simple formal procedures for routine processes. In addition, she tried to schedule Ebby's time more efficiently by minimizing impromptu meetings. Only weeks after she began, she proved indispensible. Ebby invited her to join the office full-time.

Mary Frances agreed, with one proviso—she would continue her studies in night school until she earned her degree from SMU. She quickly created a place for herself within the organization. She established office management routines and stuck to them. She kept the business records up to date and identified clearly delineated responsibilities. One of her most challenging projects was to help organize the Multiple Listing Service materials. The MLS was basically a collection of five-by-seven sheets with price, size, location and other information on one side and a photograph of the home on the other side. After the initial booklet was distributed to all member brokers, keeping track of changes was nearly impossible. Each week, updates to the MLS material were distributed via "hot sheets," several loose leaf pages mailed to area brokers. In most cases, the hot sheets contained price changes, pending sales, and other information critical to closing a sale. The challenge was collating the information on the hot sheet with the most recently published MLS sheets.

If an agent spotted a home in the MLS booklet, she would have no way of knowing if the price had changed, for example, without searching through several weeks' worth of hot sheets. This was a tedious proposition and routinely subject to error. One of Mary Frances's early tasks was to update the MLS packet of information of any price changes based on the weekly hot sheets. She devised a simple, methodical system of recording updated information that made locating current information practically foolproof. Agents loved the new system, which meant they received better information faster and could spend their time with current clients or prospecting for new clients.

In addition to the MLS update project, Mary Frances had a range of duties. She greeted walk-in customers, answered Ebby's mail while she was out of town, and kept Ebby informed about the office while she was away. Ebby received a vast amount of mail. In order to respond as quickly as possible, Mary Frances got in the habit of drafting replies for Ebby's approval. This seemingly straightforward task was an invaluable time-saver. What made the task even easier was that Mary Frances had a way with words. Her written work was clear, to the point, and creative. So good, in fact, that she took on new duties editing the agents' listing information submitted to the MLS system. A "small house" became a "cottage." A "must-see" was transformed into "beautifully appointed." "Large yard" became "gorgeously landscaped." She used other words that she believed would attract more buyers and lead to a faster sale. Words like "handyman special" and "turnkey" and "move-in condition." Her language was something akin to commercial poetry.

Although Mary Frances had slowed the pace of her formal education, she was learning from one of the top real estate salespersons in the country. The two women spent a lot of time together. The camaraderie led Ebby to believe in and encourage Mary Frances's abilities. Ebby would often have Mary Frances type her speeches from handwritten notes. Mary Frances was able to follow Ebby's thought process, her priorities, and her overarching message. From answering mail, to writing listings, to preparing motivating sales presentations, Mary Frances received an education that would be the envy of any SMU graduate, as well as a business degree just a few semesters later than planned.

To say all this hard work early in her career paid off would be an understatement. In 1979, Mary Frances became Executive Vice President and General Sales Manager of Ebby Halliday Realtors. Ten years later, in 1989, she was named President. In some ways, Mary Frances's early career was similar to Ebby's. The decision to take a full-time job with Ebby's growing company was one of the soundest career decisions of her life, a decision not unlike Ebby's resolve to leave Omaha and move to Dallas.

## RELYING ON GOOD JUDGMENT

In 1937, Ebby accepted the promotion to manage Consolidated's Dallas location.

Given what little information she had at the time, her decision was formed more by a gut feeling—an unconscious judgment—

than by a reasoned assessment of the facts. She did have some information. At the library, Ebby looked through newspapers and magazine articles and gleaned that Dallas was large and prosperous. At a minimum, the new manager position would give her a chance to test her selling skills in a larger market. What she didn't fully understand was just how different two cities could be. Omaha was quiet. Dallas was noisy. Omaha was about corn. Dallas was about oil. All told, Omaha was sedate, while Dallas was booming and exuberant.

Two years earlier, Dallas had sponsored the Texas Centennial Exposition marking one hundred years of Texas's independence from Mexico. President Franklin Roosevelt visited the exposition and announced that the Centennial was not just for Texans; it was for all citizens of this great nation. More than 6.3 million visitors strolled down the midway. At one event, movie star Joan Crawford showed off her commission as captain of the Texas Rangerettes. At another, a cowboy sat atop Hell's a-Poppin' Plymouth, a car rigged so the cowboy sitting in the saddle on the hood could drive. The midway included the famous "Streets of Paris" exhibit, the Rocket Ride rollercoaster, and the "Original Texas Snake Farm" tent show. Less adventurous types could slip next door to a concession booth for a cold Dr Pepper.

The Centennial was a turning point for Dallas. Gone were the days of cattle drives and saloons prominently listed in the Chamber of Commerce material. Dallas had transformed itself into a modern industrial powerhouse. In the process, the city and its citizens had become the poster child for Roosevelt's New Deal programs— businesses were expanding, the unemployed found work, and people were spending rather than saving. The Centennial planners had spent millions of dollars to get the exposition ready. In return, millions of visitors flocked to the event.

Another major event of the 1930s set Dallas apart from other cities—the discovery of oil. Speculator Columbus Marion "Dad" Joiner believed the pine trees of East Texas were hiding the largest oil reservoir on earth. He managed to acquire oil leases on more than five thousand acres in Rusk County, east of Dallas. Joiner set up drilling rigs to see what he could find. On his third attempt, he struck black gold. Within a month, the population of the nearby town of Kilgore swelled from 700 to 10,000 people, and Joiner got his nickname "Dad" for fathering the East Texas oil field.

News of Joiner's discovery brought out old creditors, and to settle at least some of his debts, he agreed to sell a portion of his leases to Haroldson Lafayette Hunt, Jr., for $30,000 in cash, with the balance of approximately $1.3 million payable over time. Within a few years, the enormous expanse of the East Texas oil field had been mapped. The underground oil field covered an area forty-five miles long and three to twelve miles wide. Dallas became a convenient headquarters for independent producers, wildcatters, investors, pipeline operators, oil-well scouts, and drilling contractors. At the same time, oil revenues poured into Dallas.

When Ebby stepped off the train in 1938, she was amazed. Cars and trucks lined the streets. Busses zoomed past. People filled the sidewalks. As she pushed her way to the bus stop, she thought briefly of walking the twelve blocks to the W.A. Green Department Store. Given the traffic, the walk might very well be faster. The store was located at the intersection of Main Street and Ervay Street. It wasn't far and it was easy to find. What changed her mind was the heat. The temperature in Dallas was stifling.

The Nebraska summers had been hot, but at least there was a breeze.

She climbed aboard a bus and stood in the aisle, one hand on her handbag and the other on the back of a nearby seat. As the bus turned east onto Main, Ebby was impressed with how new and well organized the city appeared. She watched the people on the street. Compared to the unhurried pace of Omahans, Dallasites were in a race. Everyone seemed to be on a mission, a salesman heading to his next appointment, a woman on a shopping trip; each person moved at hasty, almost reckless speeds. As the bus inched deeper into downtown, Ebby noticed another difference. The clothes were newer, more tailored. The men's shirts were whiter, with more starch. The women's dresses were more stylish. Better yet, nearly everyone wore a hat.

In the midst of the traffic and noise and heat, the bus finally stopped at the corner of Main and Ervay. The doors wedged open, facing south into the massive and ornate entrance to W.A. Green's chief competitor, the legendary Neiman Marcus department store. Neiman Marcus was a larger, plusher store. It was lavish in ways she couldn't immediately describe. Peering through the glass doors, she saw a beautifully decorated sales floor with scores of shoppers. Outside, the display windows were filled with shoes, dresses, handbags, jewelry—every item a sensational piece of art stylishly orchestrated to fit within the window. She wondered how anyone could dream up the displays, much less transform them into the tangible images in front of her.

In one window, she found nothing but hats, designs she had never seen before. Never mind that many were so whimsical they might never sell, what intrigued her was the same sense of allure and high fashion that attracted other shoppers. Ebby hurried into the Neiman Marcus store, found the hat department on the third floor, and browsed. She spent the better part of an hour touching the merchandise, peeking inside hat after hat to see how things were put together, testing a brim for feel and flexibility. Ebby left the hat department and walked into the street armed with the knowledge that this was where she was meant to be. Coming to Dallas was the right thing to do.

She crossed the street and entered the Wilson Building, an eight-story brick and stone masterpiece of French ornate architecture. An arcade connected the Wilson Building to another building at the corner of Elm and Ervay that housed the W.A. Green Department Store and its hat department on the sixth floor. Ebby found the manager, a slight woman with unusually long curly hair, and introduced herself. "I'm Ebby Halliday. I believe you are expecting me."

"I'm Mae," she said. "You found us?"

Ebby glanced around the showroom. "On the sixth floor," Ebby said.

"I know what you're thinking, but don't worry. Sales are strong."

"And the customers?"

"The best you'll ever meet. I can guarantee it."

Ebby brushed at the front of her skirt. "I made a short detour across the street."

"It's impressive, don't you think? You should have been here for the Centennial. Neiman's staged a special show, 'One Hundred Years of Texas Fashion.' It was hard not to be impressed."

"How do we compete?" Ebby asked.

"We don't. Our clientele is different. You'll see."

In the days that followed, Mae made telephone calls to her steady customers, asking them to drop by the store to meet Ebby. The calls worked. Over the next two weeks, Consolidated's hat department was busy with old and new customers alike, all of them eager to try on the latest designs and talk fashion. Ebby was all of twenty-seven at the time. She was confident in her abilities. She had been through a similar move when she was transferred from Kansas City to Omaha, and she knew how to connect with people. Ebby made a few suggestions as to fit, style, color. She suggested to a tall woman with a narrow face to let her hair lie naturally over her ears. "Now tilt the hat slightly to the right. That's it. See, there you are. It looks perfect." The women instantly took to her. The hat department was located on the same floor as the finer dresses, and Ebby intuitively recommended a dress that might compliment the hat.

Mae was an unexpected blessing, doing all she could to transition Ebby into her new surroundings without missing a step. Her customers were extraordinarily loyal, and the W.A. Green store management was particularly helpful. In fact, the personnel department staff had found Ebby a room, negotiated her rent, and arranged to ship her trunks to a boarding house on Moser Avenue in East Dallas. Her room was comfortable and conveniently located near a streetcar line. The new city, faithful clients, and living quarters close to town were more than she had hoped for.

## ENLISTING OLD HABITS FOR NEW PUPOSES

Ebby's habit of success at the Herzberg store in Omaha followed her to Dallas. Sales at the Dallas location steadily improved. There were several reasons for the upward trend. One was Ebby's innate sales acumen. Others included devoted customers, well-priced merchandise, and a growing regional economy. An article in the influential *Atlantic Monthly* described Dallas as a new world, a place where the environs were fluid, and a visitor had the sensation of being in a new, strangely innocent world. The article only confirmed what Ebby observed on the day she stepped from the train—Dallas was a city unlike any other. Dallas residents were third in purchasing power behind New York and Washington, D.C. The syndicated columnist Walter Winchell called Dallas women the "best-dressed" in the nation. It didn't take Ebby long to fit right in.

In the summer of 1941, Ebby's mother, Lucille, telephoned. She explained there was an outbreak of polio in Junction City, where she now lived.

"One of the boys on the high school football team," Lucille said. "You don't know him. How could you? He died of polio a few days ago."

"How can I help?" Ebby asked. Polio was one of the most dreaded childhood diseases of the twentieth century. Epidemics crippled hundreds of young children each year.

"They shut down the school. No telling when it will open again."

"What about you?"

"Me, I'm fine. Why I called is your brother Paul."

"What about him?"

"He's in high school, on the football team." Lucille paused. "I wondered if he could stay with you for a while. Just until the school re-opens."

"Absolutely," Ebby said. She was grateful to help.

"Oh my. You don't know how much I appreciate this. I'll put him on the train. He'll be along your way day after tomorrow. Oh, and you won't recognize him."

Ebby had last seen Paul some time ago, so Lucille described exactly what he would be wearing. And Lucille was right. At the train station, Ebby realized for the first time that Paul was now a grown man, tall and wide as any college football player she had ever seen. He had changed his name from Bigler to Hanson after Lucille's divorce from Fred Bigler and subsequent marriage to Elmer Hanson. And despite the half-brother lineage, Ebby referred to him as her brother.

Paul stayed with Ebby for two months. They spent evenings catching each other up on the past nine years. During the days when Ebby was at work, Paul took the bus into downtown and went to the movies. His favorite movie house was an ancient converted vaudeville theater with its opulent decor and conditioned cool air. Between movies, he dropped into the W.A. Green store to visit his sister. After work, the two met in town and took the bus to the boarding house for dinner. Living together was a squeeze, and although her room resembled a campground with Paul's gear spread across the floor, Ebby was disappointed when Lucille called to say the high school would open up again in late October.

At the train station, they said their goodbyes.

"Don't be a stranger," she said.

"Thanks for having me. You have a good life here."

"Do you have any ideas for college? Dallas has a handful of good universities."

"I did enjoy my stay."

"Or a job. This city is growing. We'll need people willing to work."

97

"I'll think about it," Paul said. "I promise I will."

Dallas was growing. There was no denying it. The population had doubled in the last twenty years, and the rate of growth was accelerating. The challenge was to grow right along with it. And that's exactly what Ebby Halliday Realtors would do.

## EXPANDING WISELY

By 1958, Ebby Halliday Realtors had grown to thirty sales agents. In the process, the company had outgrown its office space and the main branch, now located on Northwest Highway in Preston Centor, was wall-to-wall agents. A new two-story savings and loan building planned to open in October only a block away. Ebby was a planner, but she was also accustomed to making decisions quickly. Her goal was growth, and without hesitation, she negotiated a lease in the new building as its first tenant. The new larger location would house the current residential sales agents, and the main branch would become the farm and ranch division.

The new location was office number four. The number of offices was one of many ways of keeping score in the real estate sales business. Another measure was the number of agents, but what really mattered was sales. In 1958, Ebby Halliday Realtors had sales of approximately $12 million, an impressive number given that the median home price in the Dallas area was around $24,000. Ebby's company had sold roughly five hundred homes that year. Ebby Halliday Realtors was not the top real estate office in Dallas, but if her firm continued to grow at its current pace, it soon would be.

Growth was not the only yardstick. Another measure of success was how much organizations and individuals helped improve their own communities, how much Ebby and her staff helped to enhance neighborhoods, volunteered, raised funds for worthy causes, committed to nonprofit organizations, participated in education programs, and helped sponsor grants. Expansion, revenue, and profits were important, but so was civic responsibility.

## RESOLVING TO MAKE CIVIC SERVICE A PRIORITY

Another benefit of being in town for an extended period was that Ebby could get caught up with her civic responsibilities. In Ebby's mind, *civic service* meant educating citizens about their rights and obligations in the community. She organized the Beautify Greater Dallas Association, and the group elected her as its first president. BGDA consisted of volunteers who donated their time to clean up vacant lots. Typically, the unkempt lots were along major thoroughfares. Ebby assembled a seventy-five-member advisory panel to recruit organizations and individuals within the city. The idea was that an organization would adopt a particular tract of land and help keep it clean. Another of Ebby's projects was encouraging the little league baseball team her company sponsored, a small contribution perhaps but one she enjoyed. She regularly attended games when her schedule permitted.

Without question, Ebby's highest priority project was lobbying for Dallas as host city for the 1960 National Association of Real Estate Brokers convention. Her stay at home gave her the time to make calls and rely on some of the goodwill she had accumulated in her travels around the country making speeches on behalf of the association. She could now place a call from her office and expect a call back, a near impossibility on the road, even if the caller anticipated some gentle arm-twisting for one of Ebby's pet projects. Her campaigning so far had worked. The NAREB board was prepared to give Dallas a serious shot at hosting the convention. The final decision would not be announced until November, six months away. Her telephone lobbying included calling all current NAREB board members and making her case. In addition, she set up face-to-face meetings with key brokers in San Antonio, Houston, St. Louis, Kansas City, and other cities to listen to their opinions and respond to objections. Whenever possible, she scheduled the face-to-face meetings in conjunction with her upcoming speaking schedule.

Her time at home passed quickly, and she was soon back on the road. Her first out-of-town speech in months was in Seattle. She was one of two featured speakers at the Seattle Parade of Homes kickoff dinner in September. Over six hundred real estate personnel, home builders, mortgage bankers, and title company representatives listened to Ebby's latest presentation, "New Ideas in Selling." After stops in California to visit several offices, she journeyed to Baton Rouge where she spoke to the local NAREB Women's Council. Her topic was "The Woman's Viewpoint in Buying," aimed directly at the all-female audience. Then she made her way north to Pennsylvania with several stops in between to visit more real estate offices. At the Haverford Women's Council, Ebby spoke about the role of "The Forgotten Man," describing the function men should play in the home-buying process.

Next was New York and then Boston, where she visited with local brokers about the upcoming convention. The reaction she received had been consistently positive. Everyone she spoke with seemed keenly interested in the idea. After completing her East Coast swing, she returned to Dallas to prepare for the annual convention.

Ebby arranged her return to coincide with the grand opening of her fourth office. The new space had been worth the wait. The office was filled with color, the conference room was an impressive centerpiece, and fresh plants added to the comfortable atmosphere. The client reception area was designed specifically to put clients in a positive attitude, and a unique lighting arrangement gave the office a feel of efficiency and hominess. Ebby moved her office to the new building and was excited to get down to business.

Her business was growing, and it was time to take advantage of that momentum. She was convinced that hosting the 1960 convention would be good for Dallas. The convention meant media exposure for the city, income for local businesses, and ultimately more home buyers for Ebby Halliday Realtors. To make it happen, Ebby and thirty other real estate professionals agreed to make the trip to Toronto where, if the summer-long lobbying effort proved successful, Dallas would be named the host city for the 1960 National Association of Real Estate Brokers convention.

Shortly after the group arrived in Toronto, one of them learned that no opposition had emerged at the board level. The announcement was pending, but it looked like a lock. On the next-to-last day of the convention, the chairman announced that Dallas had been selected to host the 1960 NAREB national convention. Ebby's efforts had paid off in recognition for her, her company, and her city.

# CHAPTER EIGHT
## Connecting Pays Dividends

All of Ebby's hard work had paid off. Dallas would be the host city for the 1960 National Association of Real Estate Brokers convention. Perhaps the only people more pleased with the announcement than those in real estate were business owners, especially those of hotels, motels, and restaurants who could look forward to thousands of Dallas visitors flooding the city in November.

In 1960, Ebby set new goals for herself. At the top of her list was building a formal real estate referral network throughout the country. The project would take time, and she cut back her travel plans and speaking schedule for weeks and months at a stretch. She had been working on the project part-time for the last six months. The project was sponsored by Ebby and three other Realtors—Gordon Williamson from Detroit, Max Moore from Denver, and Bob Walker from Indianapolis—all well known in their markets. They came up with the idea, a venture they had been discussing at the meetings of the Brokers Institute, a committee of the National Association of Real Estate Boards.

In her travels since, she had serendipitously created an informal broker network of her own. When a client planned a move from Dallas to some other city, Ebby made a few calls and put her clients in contact with a broker office or individual agent in that new city. The problem was that Ebby didn't know everybody. She didn't know an agent, for example, in every town in America. A formal referral network could fill in the gaps by connecting selected brokers across the country.

A referral network would provide home buyers with information about professional real estate firms in other cities. Network members, the way the four founders saw it, could handle all a home buyer's real estate needs—selecting a general location, previewing properties, finding schools, arranging financing, and negotiating—on a one-stop basis. Initially, only one or two firms from each city would be selected to participate in the new program. The idea was that a broker who handled the home sale in one city would refer the client to a broker in the destination city and receive a commission for the referral.

From the home seller's perspective, the process made selecting a broker in the new city easy. The time saved in searching for an agent could be used to find a new house. Because Ebby wanted to target corporate clients who regularly transferred employees to other divisions or business units in a different city, she focused on spreading the word about the benefits to the corporation. One of the biggest benefits of the referral network was saving money. By allowing an agent to preview properties before buyers even visited the new city, an agent could shorten the buying process considerably, thus saving the cost of temporary housing. Ebby and her committee imposed other measures intended to ensure that all transactions met a high ethical standard. One of those standards required all network members to be members of the National Association of Real Estate Boards and agree to adhere to the organization's code of conduct.

In May, Ebby flew to Chicago for the NAREB annual meeting. She was Chairman of the Convention Committee for the upcoming convention later that year in Dallas. Ebby's referral program partners were also in town, and the three finalized a few remaining details. They selected a name, Inter-City Real Estate Referral Service (ICRERS), and they chose officers. The committee selected Bob Walker as president, Gordon Williamson as first vice president, Jack Justice as second vice president, and Ebby Halliday as secretary. Everyone agreed that the new service would be announced that fall at the annual convention in Dallas.

## PLACING SERVICE FIRST

After the Chicago meeting, Ebby gave a talk in San Antonio. The title of her speech was "Sell Yourself First," basically a new take on an old idea—the power of a first impression, caring more about the customer than about yourself, dressing appropriately, and learning to listen. With the convention approaching, Ebby squeezed in three more appearances in Cincinnati, Grand Rapids, and Pittsburgh. In Pittsburgh, she spoke to the newly-formed Greater Pittsburgh Chapter of the Women's Council. Her speech that evening was titled "Act Like a Lady, Do Business Like a Man," and it contained much of the advice she had given to other chapters in the past couple of years. She added a new refrain. She told the group that successful women had made headway in the profession by not exhibiting a "women are better than men" attitude. "Do the best job you can do," she told the audience. "Be exceptional, in fact, and let your success change public opinion." Ebby sought to empower women by encouraging them to commit to hard work. Instant success was a false promise. She persuaded her audience to put service before commissions. But first, she said, "Put your home life in order so you can give the continuous drive that selling requires."

## TRADING MY HOUSE FOR YOURS

Two weeks before the NAREB convention, Ebby began composing her remarks to the opening session of the Women's Council. In 1960, residential real estate sales across the country were down 25 percent from the previous year. Sales in New England were down almost 30 percent, the West Coast 6 percent, and the South 9 percent. In addition to flagging sales, new housing starts were down 20 percent from 1.5 million the previous year to a round 1.2 million in 1960.

Ebby had been in the business long enough to bring some perspective. During the convention, she told the audience that the ups and downs were all a part of the inevitable real estate cycle. The market had switched from a seller's market to a buyer's market. In Ebby's view, the only thing that had changed was how hard an agent had to work to stay even and how creative an agent had to be to maintain consistent sales. Hard work and creativity were a couple of the trade's requisite skills that everyone in attendance should be practicing anyway. Looking ahead, Ebby anticipated the "Baby Boom" market would materialize in 1965 and would likely lead to two million new housing starts per year.

One of the hot topics at the 1960 convention was residential real estate "trades"—that is, trade-in of houses. In many ways, the process was similar to trading in your old car for a new one. A customer might be ready to buy a new house, but only if he could get rid of the old house. The way these trades worked in 1960 was that a buyer located a home in a new development, the development owner or builder would contact a real estate agency, which would send an appraiser to value the buyer's trade-in home. The Realtor would typically offer the buyer 85 percent to 90 percent of the trade-in's appraised value. The Realtor would pay the buyer with the proceeds of a short-term loan arranged by the Federal National Mortgage Association, known as "Fannie Mae." The Realtor then owned the house. If all went as planned, the Realtor would later sell the house for at least the appraised value and pocket a profit after paying off the loan.

Of the five hundred real estate professionals in Dallas, only fifty to seventy-five were set up to accept trade-ins. Ebby Halliday Realtors was ahead of the game. Ebby and her staff were already heavily involved in the trade-in business, having handled over two hundred transactions the previous year. Profits from Ebby Halliday Realtors' trade-in business totaled 25 percent of company profit.

Ebby's trade-in program was handled by Posie Willess, a top assistant, who also managed the Forest Lane office. The trade-in business was not without its risks. A couple of bad appraisals could wipe out any profits from five or more solid trade-in transactions.

When a piece of her business worked especially well, Ebby was quick to find additional related channels. The referral network service, for instance, was the perfect platform for expanding the scope of her trade-in business. When a buyer wanted to trade for a new house in the same city, the process was simple and efficient. But what if the buyer wanted to move out of town? Could he somehow get someone to take his old house in trade and get the proceeds applied to the purchase of the new house in the new city? The answer was yes, according to Ebby. It didn't matter to Ebby where the buyer purchased a new house; she simply purchased the trade-in at a discount and added another house to her inventory. The proceeds of the trade-in were transferred to the referral service member broker in the new city who would then assist the buyer in finding a new house.

With all the pieces in place, Ebby and her partners announced the formation of the Inter-City Real Estate Referral Service during the national convention. A press release noted the new referral service already had at least one leading Realtor in fifty key metropolitan areas. Ebby's idea for a nationwide relocation and referral network was finally in place. Each member had only a few responsibilities: become aware of potential corporate relocations, make the corporation aware of ICRERS' services, and provide exceptional support to the relocating corporation and its employees. Such support might include picking up home buyers at the airport for house-hunting trips, making arrangements for babysitters on such trips, and locating hotels, meals, and even entertainment.

Despite the nationwide dip in home sales, 1960 had been a good year for Ebby Halliday Realtors. Sales set another record, six agents joined the company, and Ebby accepted several new board memberships. In the coming year, she would take on the roles of regional vice president of the Farm and Land Brokers Institute, director of the Texas Real Estate Association, program chairman of the Dallas Real Estate Board, and vice-president of the North Dallas Chamber of Commerce. It had been a busy and successful year. The only thing that made it better was the confident tenor of a familiar voice.

## SHARING STORIES

Maurice and Ebby talked on the phone infrequently, yet when they did, their conversations were a sort of vacation, pensive and faraway and never disappointing. "Tell me something," she said into the phone.

"Okay," Maurice said.

"About yourself."

"I've told you most of it already."

"I don't believe that."

"Well, let me think."

"Go on. Tell me something I've never heard."

He didn't answer right away. "Did I tell you about the time in '41 that I got a call from J. Edgar Hoover?"

"Go on," she said.

And he did.

At 7:02 a.m. on December 7, 1941, a large blip appeared on a radar screen at the U.S. Army's Opana Point station, Oahu, Hawaii. The information was relayed to an information center at Pearl Harbor on the southern end of the island. Forty-two minutes later, 183 Japanese aircraft strafed air bases across Oahu Island, dropping aerial torpedoes along battleship row. At 8:54 a.m. the second wave of 170 Japanese aircraft dumped plane loads of bombs on top of naval air stations across the island. The surprise attack ended ninety minutes later with 2,386 Americans killed and 1,139 wounded.

Special Agent in Charge Maurice Acers received a telephone call from FBI Director J. Edgar Hoover on Sunday afternoon. Hoover asked if Maurice had heard about the events in Hawaii, now barely three hours old. The thirty-four-year-old Special Agent in Charge had not. Hoover wanted fifty agents from the San Antonio office to report to the FBI's San Francisco office by the following morning. Hoover gave no details about the assignment, but Maurice knew what was coming. With Japan already waging war in East Asia, the FBI had begun compiling names of U.S. residents it suspected of potential subversive acts. The Custodial Detention Index (CDI), as it was called, was a list of enemy aliens, primarily Japanese, Italian, and German. The FBI, Justice Department, and intelligence units of the armed forces had been building a list composed of influential members of the Japanese west coast community for almost three years. Administration and military leaders doubted the loyalty of ethnic Japanese. Many had been educated in Japan, where school curricula emphasized reverence for the emperor. At the core of this mistrust, they feared that Japanese living in the United States might commit acts of sabotage against civilian and military targets.

Maurice was familiar with the project. He had little doubt that his role was to help round up Japanese Americans and relocate them to special Department of Justice internment camps.

On Monday, December 8, President Roosevelt declared war on Japan. The president authorized his attorney general to arrest high-risk individuals on the CDI list. Armed with a blanket arrest warrant, the FBI seized hundreds of Japanese and Japanese Americans by the end of the day, all classified as "most dangerous" on the CDI list. The captives were held in municipal jails and prisons until moved to Department of Justice internment camps. These camps were separate from the more commonly known Japanese-American internment camps operated by the Wartime Relocation Authority, where more than 120,000 Japanese nationals and American citizens of Japanese ancestry were sent the following year. The Department of Justice internment camps functioned under far more stringent conditions and were used extensively to detain people suspected of having committed actual crimes or of harboring "enemy sympathies."

Maurice quickly delegated the job of notifying his agents to an assistant. He turned his attention to transporting the men to the west coast. He called Tom Braniff, president and founder of Braniff Airways, in Oklahoma City. Braniff agreed to provide an airplane in San Antonio later that evening to fly the agents to San Francisco.

There was widespread agreement among political and military leaders about the Japanese American internment camps. One voice of opposition, however, was J. Edgar Hoover's. Because the FBI had already arrested those he considered genuine security threats, the director felt more arrests were unnecessary. Hoover sent a memo to the attorney general in which he wrote about perceived disloyalty by Japanese Americans. He said, "Every complaint in this regard has been investigated, but in no case has any information been obtained which would substantiate the allegation." President Roosevelt and the attorney general, however, supported the military assessment. Evacuation and internment were imperative.

"Go on," Ebby said.

"That's enough for now. It's getting late," Maurice said.

"So Hoover didn't agree with the camps."

"Not the war relocation camps, he didn't."

"What did you think?"

"Perhaps we can get into that some other time."

"Parts of your life, it's like reading a novel."

"Is it a good novel?"

"I'll let you know when we get to the end."

## MAKING HISTORY

These long-distance phone conversations with Maurice were a much-needed break from Ebby's daily routine. Maurice was able to give her a perspective she wouldn't have considered otherwise. The next morning, however, it was back to work. The year 1961 started quickly for Ebby with speaking engagements in Amarillo, Longview, Fort Worth, Oklahoma City, Milwaukee, Buffalo, and Ann Arbor. Sandwiched between the Fort Worth and Oklahoma City stops, Ebby made a history-making speech to an all-male gathering at Humble Oil and Refining Company. The company's 1961 annual convention was the first time a woman delivered the keynote to what was considered a bunch of hard-nosed service station managers.

Ebby told the audience that the service station business was no different from the real estate business. In both businesses, the aim is to focus on the customer. She told them what they were selling wasn't only fuel, but the greatest commodity on earth—service. She offered the following suggestions: "Make your customers feel important. We deal in human relations. People are impressed by what they see, hear, and feel in your presence. Make your customers feel they are your most important customer. Sell them on the value of your product. And," she cautioned, "don't knock the competitor's product. Let it knock itself."

She had a list of other ideas that had nothing to do with oil or real estate and everything to do with what she saw as growing government interventionism. She suggested taking a firm stand on current issues. "Protect your own liberties by being actively interested in your community. Voice your opinion when the government interferes with those things you can do for yourself. Be proud of the American system of business, which offers each of you the opportunity to be your own boss. And last, use your initiative on a daily basis to increase your business."

In recounting Ebby's presentation in a subsequent issue of the *Humble Sales Lubricator* newsletter, the editor noted, "Even a misogynist would agree that Ebby Halliday was perfect for the job."

## TAKING SIDES

During a subsequent speech to members of the Alabama Real Estate Association, Ebby followed her own advice. She took a stand. At a noon luncheon, Senator John Sparkman from Alabama told the convention that the Housing Act of 1961 was the most comprehensive piece of housing legislation ever passed by

Congress. Its major programs included mortgage insurance, urban renewal, college housing, and low-rent public housing. He said it ranked second only to the Housing Act of 1949, a comprehensive expansion of the federal role in mortgage insurance and public housing. At a dinner speech that evening, Ebby said she didn't agree. "Private businesses, not the government, can do the job much better and pay taxes while doing it." She told the group that the federal government had shown an increasing trend toward socialism in its housing programs. In her opinion, this was an alarming development. And worse, government often saddled a community with help it did not want and did not need.

After Alabama, she had speaking engagements in Delaware, Ohio, and later Miami. In November at the NAREB national convention in Miami, Ebby accepted a three-year term as a director of the American Chapter of the International Real Estate Federation. In 1962, after speaking in a handful of Texas cities, she was off to Honolulu, Atlanta, Nashville, and Pittsburgh. Her topic at each venue was "Let's Close the Sale," which consisted of advice for getting buyers and sellers to agree. At its root, Ebby's talk was about ways to avoid and resolve conflict. Her remarks were influenced, at least in part, by events taking place at the national and international level, most notably, the Cuban Missile Crisis.

On October 14, 1962, U.S. reconnaissance photographs revealed missile bases being built in Cuba in response to similar U.S. bases built along the Turkish-Soviet border. Two weeks later, President John F. Kennedy and Soviet General Secretary Nikita Khrushchev agreed to withdraw their respective nuclear missiles, although only the Soviet removal was made public. For most Americans, the United States appeared to have won the confrontation.

A short two weeks later, Ebby spoke in Detroit and noted that the collective apprehension of the nation had eased considerably. She participated in a Women's Council panel entitled "Tools, Tactics, and Techniques," and later a round table discussion of "What Government Wants to Do and Industry Ought to Do for Farm Prosperity." As a panel member, she urged farm brokers to keep informed on farm programs and to make their views known on proposed government programs.

In reference to the administration's recent remarks about a rural area crisis, Ebby noted that advocates of federal farm controls overlooked the fact that the farmer was squarely in a fix. Excess federal meddling had consistently worsened farm economics rather than improved them. Ebby feared the term "rural renewal" was gaining favor in government circles. "If rural renewal becomes popular, it's likely to be compared to urban renewal. Advocates in Congress can then say, 'Look at how rural renewal lags behind urban renewal. It's obvious that America's rural renewal programs are underfunded.' The next step is government-funded grants to local rural redevelopment agencies," she warned. The solution, Ebby pointed out, was new and creative approaches to revitalizing farm areas without governmental subsidies. She called upon agencies specializing in farm properties to take the initiative in developing such creative approaches. During the convention, she accepted three more offices for the coming year: regional vice president and member of the board of governors for the Farm Brokers Institute, and regional vice president of the National Institute of Real Estate Brokers.

In May 1963, Ebby spoke in Chicago at the International Real Estate Federation, the international equivalent of NAREB. The meeting marked the first time the annual event had been held outside Europe. Ebby participated in a panel discussion. Of the nine participants, she was the only woman. She said, "To have a successful career in real estate, a woman must be organized, be willing to set personal emotions aside, and be willing to learn."

A month later, she received one of the crowning achievements of her career. Ebby Halliday was named "Texas Realtor of the Year" by the Texas Real Estate Association in Galveston. By way of congratulations, Ebby received several lengthy telegrams, but it was one of the shortest that stood out. It read, "It's about time, Honey." It had taken forty-two years for the good ole boys from Texas to select a woman as Realtor of the Year.

# CHAPTER NINE
## Thriving on Change

At a speech to the National Association of Insurance Women, Ebby spoke about empowering women. "It isn't the meek who seem to be inheriting the earth—it's the women. Women own two-thirds of all U.S. assets. We own $80 billion in life insurance, amounting to 75 percent of all life insurance in force. Life insurance payouts to widows amount to $15 billion a year. We women pay almost 80 percent of all estate and inheritance taxes." To drive home her point, she said that women own 51 percent of all stock,

50 percent of all savings, 53 percent of all government bonds, and 45 percent of all mortgages. "And it's not all inherited wealth I'm talking about," she said. "One in three American women works outside of the home."

She noted that without women, Congress would have seventeen empty seats and state legislatures 347 vacant chairs. Banks would shut their doors because six thousand women were bank officers. Schools would close because 1.5 million women were educating America's children. And the government would grind to a halt because 2.25 million government employees were women. Women voters outnumbered men by four million. "Women have a marvelous opportunity to stand up and be heard," she said. "They, we, must stand tall and make our case. Women have the power to stem the rising tide of socialism and the growth of the welfare state. A woman's vote can preserve our fundamental principles and our way of life. We must resist, by our vote, the drift toward an all-powerful central government. We must, while being aware of our problems at home and abroad, also assess our values. Analyze what made us strong, free, and democratic in the first place. We must redouble our efforts at home, in our cities, and in our states to stand on principles and not expediency. We must not look to Washington for all the answers. Rather, look to our own actions, thoughts, and voting record to send representatives to Washington who reflect the principles that have made America the freest of all nations."

## MOBILIZING CREATIVITY

Ebby's rousing speech was more than a pep talk. It was heartfelt. Women could and should make a difference in the workplace, in their communities, and in the country's governance. Ebby had worked all her life, and she knew what women were capable of, especially when things got tough.

In 1941, when Maurice received his phone call from FBI Director J. Edgar Hoover, Ebby was managing the Consolidated Millinery's showroom on the sixth floor of the W.A. Green department store in Dallas. On December 8th, the *Dallas Morning News* headline read simply, "War." The Japanese had attacked Pearl Harbor, Malaya, Hong Kong, Guam, the Philippines, Wake Island, and Midway Island.

Within hours, military recruiting offices in Dallas were flooded with volunteers who wanted to enlist. The local Navy recruiting office went on a twenty-four-hour, six-day schedule, with eight hours on Sunday. The Army announced it would accept men up to thirty-six years old, with an increase to fifty if the enlistee had a skilled trade. By the end of the week, recruiting offices throughout the country set new records.

With such a large male population headed to war, women began entering the workforce in large numbers. In Dallas alone, more than fifty-five thousand jobs were created to manufacture war goods, many of those jobs going to women. North American Aviation employed as many as thirty thousand workers to produce B-24 bombers, P-51 Mustangs, and AT-6 Texan trainers. New paychecks for women meant a newfound source of spending power. Nearly overnight, women became a powerful economic force in the new wartime economy.

To boost food supplies, the government encouraged citizens to plant Victory Gardens and grow extra food for the troops. Ebby's landlord at the boarding house in Dallas planted a garden, and

Ebby applied her considerable farming skills to tending it. By the end of the war, there would be twenty million gardens providing 40 percent of the country's non-military population with vegetables.

Shortly after the attack on Pearl Harbor, certain items of clothing were subject to rationing. Ladies' hats were not among them. Ebby still had a job because people continued to buy hats. Selling hats wasn't easy in wartime. Orders for her expensive ten-dollar hats dwindled to nothing. On the other hand, Ebby sold scores of two-dollar and five-dollar hats. More women were working, and more women needed sturdy, inexpensive hats. From Ebby's perspective, this wasn't a time to bury her head and hope for the best. It was, if anything, an opportunity to be creative.

Ebby wasn't certain, but she thought she might be getting customers who previously shopped only at upscale Neiman-Marcus across the street. To make her new shoppers feel at home, Ebby routinely slipped into Neiman's hat department at lunch. She examined the latest designs, returned to her showroom, and sketched a similar design, adding some unique flair or accent. She handed the drawing to her hatmaker, Pearl Kemendo, and Pearl worked her magic. Government rationing and a general cutback on spending may have affected other departments within the W.A. Green department store, but Consolidated Millinery wasn't one of them. Far from watching her sales fall, Ebby saw sales continue to grow.

## CAPITALIZING ON CORPORATE TRANSFERS

In 1963, Ebby headed to her favorite venue, New York City, for the annual NAREB convention. She co-moderated a discussion on "Service Today, Sales Tomorrow." In her introductory remarks, she noted that almost six million people had moved between states the previous year. "Add to that the number moving between cities within a state, and you get some idea of the mobility of home owners. The transfer of corporate executives and other personnel accounts for a large portion of this mobility. To help with the move, many corporations have policies to take over the employee's house, the mortgage, and other financial responsibilities once the employee accepts a transfer. These corporations typically call on us, real estate professionals, to be responsible for the home's maintenance and sale. In handling these increasingly complex 'sell and buy' situations, and in serving today's well informed buyers and sellers, our level of service becomes the key to our success."

Ebby was, in effect, describing the Inter-City Real Estate Referral Service. In the previous three years, the ICRERS had grown from fifty to 215 member firms around the country.

A week later, on November 22, 1963, President John F. Kennedy was assassinated in Dallas. In this tragic and uncertain atmosphere, Dallas could be smeared with the taint of the president's death, and executives might rethink any corporate relocations to Dallas. In response, Ebby doubled her efforts, acting as ambassador for the city and serving in her role as vice president of the North Dallas Chamber of Commerce. Ebby believed it was more important than ever to accept out-of-town speaking engagements. And the invitations continued to arrive.

During the first half of the following year, she spoke in Baltimore, Philadelphia, Omaha, New Haven, Shreveport, St. Louis, El Paso, Waco, and Midland. Initially, she was concerned that audiences might be standoffish over the assassination in Dallas and the ongoing Warren Commission investigation, but they were just as receptive and enthusiastic as they had always been.

The year 1964 also marked the acquisition of Ebby's landmark office at the northwest corner of Preston Road and Northwest Highway. The building itself had a unique look to it. The design was Connecticut Colonial-style with a symmetrical front of white clapboard and black shutters, a steeply pitched roof, and two tall chimneys poking through the ridgeline. The use of a house as an office in an otherwise residential neighborhood had been grandfathered into the zoning ordinance years earlier. When Ebby installed a sign at the new location, the residents filed a complaint. It turned out that local zoning didn't allow freestanding commercial signs, and Ebby promptly removed the sign. Signage, however, was critical to Ebby's business, and it occurred to her that the roof of her office might make an even better advertisement. The building's roof resembled a leaning billboard and supported an even larger sign than she originally intended. Once the sign went up, drivers approaching the busy intersection saw the name Ebby Halliday Realtors in white, two-foot-tall letters stylishly painted onto the roof of the house.

## COLLABORATING WITH FAMILY

Also in 1964, Ebby's brother, Paul Hanson, joined the firm. That Paul was even available to join the firm was a minor miracle. His journey from Kansas to Dallas had taken an east-west route rather than the logical north-south path. When Ebby put Paul on the train in Dallas in 1941 to return to Kansas, she didn't dream it would be another four years until she saw him again. Paul joined the Marines in January of 1943. Three months later, he found himself in the South Pacific on the island of Guadalcanal, training for the invasion of Bougainville, another island in the Solomons chain. From there it was on to the Battle of Guam and the Battle of Okinawa, the bloodiest of the Pacific War. More than 26,000 Americans were killed in the three battles. After two and a half years, a promotion to sergeant, and a commendation for meritorious service, Paul was reassigned to Camp Lejeune, North Carolina, where he was stationed when the atomic bomb brought a sudden end to the war.

Faced with the prospect of staying in the Marines or being discharged, Paul opted for the latter and headed to Kansas via Dallas to see Ebby before settling back into Junction City. Thanks to Ebby, Paul never made it home. She convinced him that he could get a fine education using his GI Bill benefits at SMU, where he promptly enrolled for the fall semester. En route to a business degree, Paul became a two-sport letterman and played on the school's baseball team with Doak Walker, SMU's four-sport letterman and two-time Heisman Trophy winner.

Like his journey to Dallas, Paul's arrival at Ebby Halliday Realtors was also roundabout. After graduating in 1949, Paul worked for Oil Well Supply, a division of U.S. Steel. Staying with the company meant a transfer to Houston to continue his advancement. Paul, his wife Fran, and their three daughters were not pleased with the idea of leaving Dallas. Paul didn't want to move, but at forty-one, he couldn't simply abandon his career just to stay in Dallas. Reluctantly, he asked Ebby to sell his house, but rather than do as he asked, she recruited her brother into the real estate business. The network referral business was growing rapidly, and a full-time person with logistical skills was badly needed.

For Ebby, 1964 was a good year. She opened two new offices, one that would become her signature location; the network referral service grew faster than she had imagined; Paul joined the firm; and the city suffered minimal economic backlash from the assassination. That same year, she was awarded Realtor of the Year by the Dallas Real Estate Board, the first woman to receive the award in the organization's forty-seven-year history. Ebby graciously accepted a giant sterling silver chalice called the Easterwood Cup, and at the ceremony commented, "If Colonel Easterwood made any mistake when he set up this award, it was in not providing a hundred such cups. There are at least a hundred Dallas Realtors equally deserving of such an award every year."

## TAKING ADVANTAGE OF TALENT

Sharing the news of her award gave Ebby an excuse to call Maurice. He was a private person. Getting to know him took time, and yet in each conversation, she learned one or two more pieces of the puzzle that was Maurice Acers. On a recent call, he had told her about a promotion in 1943.

World War II was still going strong when FBI Director Hoover tapped Maurice to return to Washington as Director of Personnel. Hoover wanted Maurice to formalize the bureau's human relations function. The bureau had grown by 75 percent in the previous two years without shoring up its procedures or processes for managing and keeping track of its people. Relying on his experience at Scotland Yard and in reviewing field office procedures, Maurice applied his organizational talents to bringing order to the chaos.

After two years in Washington, Maurice was ready for the field again. He had friends in San Antonio, and deep down that's where he wanted to settle. Whether it was by luck or by some higher-up intervening on his behalf, a job as Special Agent in Charge of the San Antonio office soon opened. The timing was perfect. The bureau's personnel department was running smoothly, its hiring frenzy was over, and the war had finally ended.

Although Maurice returned to the same office he had left two years earlier, he did so with a different perspective. He had a newfound understanding of what it meant to be the Special Agent in Charge. The human resource assignment in Washington had put him in contact with top-ranking agents in every office in the country. He learned that the job of special agent was as much about building relationships within the community as it was about performing administrative duties. The best leaders delegated routine functions to promising subordinates and spent their own time meeting local elected officials, community leaders, police, and sheriff staff.

He immediately reestablished his church affiliation and visited civic clubs, chambers of commerce, law enforcement offices, and any organization that promoted the general good of the public welfare. There was a chance that all his efforts to put down roots would be wasted if the bureau needed him elsewhere. All he could do was to follow his instincts, and his instincts said to get out and meet as many people as possible.

Two years later, Maurice received a call from Hoover. The Director wanted Maurice to consider a new post, Special Agent in Charge of a larger office, an office that, according to Hoover, needed new leadership. The transfer was a promotion; Maurice understood that. He wasn't naïve about such things, but he also understood that an offer was as good as an order. The bureau counted on its key staff to take assignments as they were handed out. Refusing a transfer was tantamount to resigning.

It was time Maurice made a decision—was he in for the long haul, or was this the time to get out? There was no question of his loyalty to the FBI. He had relocated ten times in thirteen years. The bureau had been his only job after graduating from law school. If he stayed another seven years, he could retire on a government pension. Stay, and he was guaranteed more transfers. The only way out of that cycle was to land a permanent job at headquarters in Washington, but even that didn't appeal to him. Maurice was turning forty that year, and as time slipped away, a long-term government job had one additional drawback—there was no chance of becoming wealthy on a civil servant's salary. There were other considerations. Maurice's father, Ed, was ill and dying in Dallas. Commuting between San Antonio and Dallas on weekends was relatively easy. Commuting from his next stop wouldn't be so easy. The timing and circumstances were tipping the scales in favor of leaving the FBI.

## PLANNING FOR SERENDIPITY

There was one additional factor that played into Maurice's career decision. Maurice returned to San Antonio in 1945. Around that same time, Major Allan Shivers returned from the war. Allan and Maurice had been classmates at the University of Texas law school. Back in 1934, Shivers, an ambitious new attorney from Port Arthur, Texas, managed to get himself elected to the state senate at the age of twenty-seven, the youngest member to serve in that body. In 1937, he married Marialice Shary of Mission, Texas. Shivers resigned his senate seat in 1943 to join the military, where he served with the Allied Military Government in North Africa, Italy, France, and Germany. In his time in the armed forces, he collected five battle stars and the Bronze Star.

Shortly after Shivers returned from the war in 1945, his father-in-law, John H. Shary, passed away. Shary was a prominent citrus grower, cattleman, banker, and real estate developer in the Rio Grande Valley. After his death, his son-in-law, Shivers, was named general manager of the vast Shary holdings.

In early 1946, Maurice set up a meeting with Shivers. The two reminisced about law school, and Maurice talked about his assignments with the FBI. After the meeting, months passed, and then shortly after winning the election for Lieutenant Governor of Texas, Shivers called. With less time on his hands to manage the family business, Shivers, lieutenant governor-elect, suggested that Maurice help him manage the Shary estate and its fourteen separate enterprises.

Shary headquarters was located in the small town of Mission, Texas, about five miles from the Mexican border. Life in Mission would definitely be a change of pace for Maurice. If he didn't want to be mistaken for an undertaker, he'd have to be rid of his dark suits, white shirts, and French cuffs, and grab a pair of cowboy boots and Wranglers.

The Shary holdings were even larger than Maurice had anticipated. John Shary, a young pharmacist from Omaha, had built an empire in the Rio Grande Valley. When he first visited the area, Shary was so impressed by a small crop of grapefruit raised by early citrus experimenters that he believed it was the crop of the future. Two years later, he bought sixteen thousand acres of useless brush land near the town of Mission. After setting up an irrigation system with water from the Rio Grande River, he proceeded to grow his first crop of grapefruit. Shary's prediction was dead-on. He could and did sell trainloads of grapefruit.

In part to raise capital, he developed forty-acre citrus farms, complete with the needed irrigation, and then sold or leased the land to farmers or citrus growers. Using the proceeds, Shary acquired additional acreage and developed the first commercial-scale citrus orchard. A few years later, he built the area's first modern commercial packing plant. Growers delivered the fruit, had it graded, packed, sold, and shipped in a single process.

By 1924, there were two million citrus trees in the Rio Grande Valley. Shary went on to acquire almost fifty thousand contiguous acres of land, which he named Sharyland, and developed massive groves of citrus trees. In addition to the citrus business, Shary acquired a newspaper, banks, and other financial institutions. This was the collection of assets John Shary left to his wife and daughter when he passed away in 1945 and which his son-in-law, Allan Shivers, was tasked with managing.

Maurice got busy in Mission, tending to the substantial business of John Shary's estate. At the same time, Allan Shivers was busy in Austin, tending to the not insubstantial business of the state of Texas. In his tenure as lieutenant governor, Shivers is credited with significantly strengthening the powers of the office. Together with Governor Beauford H. Jester, Shivers initiated the practice of appointing senators to specific committees and setting the daily agenda. Subsequently, the Senate passed a right-to-work law, reorganized the public school system, appropriated funds for higher education, and provided monies for improvements of state hospitals and highways.

During the legislative sessions, Shivers would return to Mission as often as possible. Once the sessions were over, he resumed the work of managing the operations of Sharyland. In the meantime, Maurice had given managers more responsibility and authority. The result was an efficient operation that needed little day-to-day supervision on his part and would need even less of the lieutenant governor's time. Perfect timing, as it turned out. On a Sunday evening in July, Governor Jester boarded the train in Austin for an overnight trip to Galveston for a routine physical checkup at the University of Texas Medical School. The following morning, a porter discovered that Governor Jester had died in his sleep of a heart attack. Four days later, Lieutenant Governor Allan Shivers was sworn in as the state's thirty-sixth governor, and Maurice Acers found himself working for the governor of Texas.

# CHAPTER TEN
## Valuing Advisors

Upon assuming office, Governor Allan Shivers gave his now famous "Goat Speech" to members of the state legislature. In it, he characterized Texas as "First in oil and last in mental hospitals. First in goats and last in care for state wards." Members responded to Shivers's political hectoring by approving tax increases and new appropriations for colleges and hospitals. Later that fall, Shivers won election to his first full term as governor. In the next legislative session, he asked for even more funds to improve roads, schools, prisons, and services for the mentally handicapped. The governor was defying conventional wisdom by raising taxes. He was also doing right by the citizens of his state.

By the end of the 1951 legislative session, Shivers had accomplished his goals. He had fully transitioned into the governor's seat, funded badly needed programs, and worked with Maurice to get the Shary estate in tip-top order.

## ANTICIPATING THE UNEXPECTED

Maurice loved the Rio Grande Valley—the geography, the community, and the people. On the other hand, there was one aspect of life in south Texas he didn't like—the uncertainty of the weather. The only thing capable of killing a citrus crop was sub-freezing temperatures, and there hadn't been a hard freeze in the valley for fifty years. Such a streak of good luck was bound to be broken, and in January 1949, a hard freeze hit the valley, with temperatures dropping to 24 degrees. Most of the citrus trees lived, though many were badly damaged when water inside the fruit, leaves, and twigs froze, rupturing cell membranes. It would take the industry a couple of years to get back to normal. Two years to the day of the 1949 freeze, the worst cold wave since the 1800s plunged into the valley, bringing with it forty-eight hours of sub-freezing temperatures. Valley towns recorded lows of 20 degrees. Three quarters of the citrus groves were wiped out.

After surveying the damage in early February, Maurice placed a call to Austin.

He said, "Governor, we've frozen our assets off down here."

Shivers had been monitoring the situation for both the citrus industry and his family's holdings. The call only confirmed what he already suspected. "I appreciate the call."

"We've got split bark, pitted fruit, and leaves without any structure. It's not good."

"How much can be saved?"

"Some. It's hard to tell, at this point. There's a lot of leaf death."

"It's time to replant, then."

"I'd say so."

"Okay, then. Can I ask you to prepare a plan, a schedule for replanting, forecasts for labor and other costs, that sort of thing? We'll be all right. I'll see what the state can do for other growers in the valley."

"I'm way ahead of you," Maurice said.

"There's one other thing," Shivers said. As head of the Democratic Party in Texas, Shivers was consumed by meetings and state functions. It was time to put some of Maurice's skills to work in Austin. He said, "Go ahead and line up the people you need to take over the replanting operation down there. There's more work up here than both of us can do."

Maurice had mixed emotions about leaving Mission. He was president of the Texas Citrus Fruit Growers Exchange. He had established his church membership in McAllen, a town six miles to the east. He was teaching men's Sunday school to fifty or more members. Occasionally, he would take the pulpit and give a sermon during Sunday service. He was also a member of Rotary International, an organization he admired. He was a believer in the Rotary's principles, its ethics, and especially the organization's Four-Way Test. For a Rotarian, any action must be preceded by four questions: Is it the truth? Is it fair to all concerned? Will it build goodwill and better friendships? Will it be beneficial to all concerned? After four and half years, Maurice held a perfect attendance record at the weekly meetings, and he would miss the organization.

On the other hand, maybe a move to Austin was what he needed. It would take time for the new trees to produce, and as a result, the fruit growers exchange wouldn't be busy for a while. And, of course, there was nothing to prevent another cold spell from setting in. Maurice and Governor Shivers agreed September was a good time for the move.

## CLAIMING STATES' RIGHTS

Returning to Austin was something of a triumph for Maurice. Twenty years earlier, he had spent three years in law school, working between classes and studying at night. The capitol, where his new office was located, was only a half-mile south of the UT law school. Part of Maurice's new duties included making appearances for the governor. Maurice's speaking ability and good looks made him the perfect stand-in for presenting awards and proclamations to individuals and cities around the state. These assignments also served a second purpose. Maurice was gauging public opinion on issues troubling the governor.

Shivers, a conservative Democrat, was drifting away from the national Democratic Party, and he wanted Maurice's advice on what mattered most to Texans. President Truman, also a Democrat, had come under increasing fire from the conservative wing of the party. Accusers blamed the president of going soft on communism and being overly committed to fighting a no-win war in Korea. The key issue for Governor Shivers was neither communism nor Korea. It was control of the tidelands, the 2.4 million acres of submerged land off the coast of the Gulf of Mexico. What made the tidelands significant was that the area was rich with oil. For one hundred years, Texas held rights to the land, but with the discovery of oil, the federal government made a claim of national ownership. A statewide poll in 1949 concluded that Texas citizens considered the tidelands the most important public issue facing the state, and Maurice concurred.

In 1949, President Truman made a play for control of the Texas tidelands. He directed the Department of Justice to sue the state of Texas to take its offshore acreage. The Supreme Court ruled in favor of the federal government in a decision that stripped the state of billions of dollars in oil leases, rentals, and royalties that had been earmarked for the Texas public school fund. By the fall of 1951, Congress had other ideas and proposed a bill to restore title to all states having submerged lands within their respective boundaries.

In a twist of fate, in the spring of 1952, Truman lost the New Hampshire primary and was forced to withdraw his reelection bid. His popularity tumbled, a direct result of his stance on the Korean War and his sacking of General Douglas McArthur. Democrat and Illinois Governor Adlai Stevenson stepped in to take Truman's place in the upcoming presidential election. Stevenson immediately announced he would veto any bill recognizing state ownership of the tidelands. Republican nominee General Dwight Eisenhower, countered by declaring his support for state ownership of the tidelands. Rather than passing a tidelands bill only to have it vetoed by Truman, congressional leaders waited for the outcome of the general election.

Upon hearing the news of Eisenhower's willingness to sign a tidelands bill, Governor Shivers hatched an audacious plan. At the state Democratic convention, he urged all members of the Texas Democratic Party to vote, not for Stevenson, a Democrat, but for Eisenhower, a Republican. Governor Shivers also cross-filed as the Republican nominee for governor in his upcoming election. Grateful for Shivers' endorsement of Eisenhower, Republican voters gave their nomination to Shivers a few weeks later, so he appeared as the gubernatorial nominee of both the Democratic Party and the Republican Party in the November 1952 general election ballot.

Shivers was reelected governor, and Eisenhower, good to his word, didn't veto the bill that restored state rights to the tidelands. In this roundabout way, Shivers got just what he wanted—Texas held onto its resource-rich tidelands. Years later, political analysts would call the Tidelands Controversy the conflict of the century between the states and the federal government.

Shortly after reelection, Governor Shivers put Maurice in charge of the clemency section of the governor's office. The position required Maurice to review pleas from inmates requesting a reduction in their prison terms. The governor's staff vetted most of the requests, and few pleas actually made it to Maurice's desk. Those that did received a thorough evaluation, including a review of the facts, the inmate's record while in prison, letters of reference, and an assortment of other documentation. Occasionally, a plea would withstand Maurice's scrutiny, and he would recommend that the governor commute the sentence.

Shivers won election to his third term as governor in November of 1954. Shortly, thereafter, he appointed Maurice to the Interstate

Oil & Gas Compact Commission, an organization comprised of governors or their representatives from oil and gas–producing states. One of the most important functions of the commission was the protection of states' rights to control oil and gas reserves within their borders. In the last four years, Maurice had honed his skills working within the bureaucracy of Texas government. He had a solid understanding of the critical issues affecting Texans, and he could anticipate roadblocks with key constituents and negotiate his way to a compromise. What he didn't anticipate was the sweeping effect of political scandal.

## READING THE SIGNS

In 1954, a newspaper reporter uncovered a scheme involving a Texas state agency known as the Veterans' Land Board. Unscrupulous real estate operators duped unsuspecting veterans into participating in a bogus land scheme. The state attorney general conducted an investigation, and by the time the investigation was complete, twenty individuals in nine counties had been indicted, including the Texas commissioner of the General Land Office on charges of conspiracy to commit theft. The commissioner received a six-year sentence in the state penitentiary at Huntsville. Despite the fact that Governor Shivers wasn't involved with the scandal, his opponents used the bad press to taint his administration.

The fact that the first state official in the history of Texas to be convicted and sentenced committed his crimes while Shivers was governor was a tremendous blow to the governor's image. It didn't matter that the commissioner was a statewide elected official rather than a Shivers appointee. The political tides were shifting, and Governor Shivers would soon leave office. As a parting gesture, he appointed Maurice to the Texas Employment Commission board in 1955. The TEC, as it was known, was the state's equivalent to the U.S. Department of Labor. Shivers believed Maurice would be a quick study and a credible member of the three-person board. Unlike commissioner positions in other state agencies, the three commissioners of the TEC were assigned to represent different constituencies: the public, labor, and employers. Maurice represented employers. The new position brought automatic access to upper level management of every company in the state.

Few people were better positioned to launch a new career at the age of forty-eight than Maurice Acers. He would be paid to serve in a role similar to that of a corporate director, which would leave him ample time to pursue other business opportunities. His position as a TEC commissioner was a perfect transition into the ranks of the self-employed. He was now free to set his own schedule and to make his own plans.

Maurice had previously invested in a beer distributorship in Beaumont, Texas. In 1957, he returned to Beaumont and invested in a savings and loan association. To keep track of his investments, he leased a suite at the Hotel Beaumont where he kept clothes and other items. In July, he strolled through the lobby and noticed a talkative crowd emerging from the hotel ballroom. A reporter was on the phone, shouting at his editor. "Save me some room on the front page of the local section. I have a great story for you. I know it was just a Lion's Club speech, but she wowed 'em."

Maurice proceeded to the driveway of the hotel where he took up his usual spot in the front passenger seat of a car waiting for passengers to the airport. A few minutes later a woman climbed into the backseat behind the driver. As the car pulled away, Maurice folded his newspaper and spoke to the driver, "It says here that Castro is still holding thirty of our Marines down there in Cuba."

The woman in the back seat spoke, Maurice rotated in his seat, and he nodded at her. "Maurice Acers," he said. "It's spelled A-C-E-R-S, but rhymes with bakers."

## PROPOSING A PARTNERSHIP

In 1965, Maurice Acers proposed marriage to Ebby Halliday. For the first time in her real estate career, Ebby disregarded her own tenets of negotiating—she accepted the first offer without making a counteroffer. For the last seven years, Ebby and Maurice had spoken often by telephone but seen each other sparingly. During the past year, Ebby noticed that Maurice's travel patterns had changed. His trips to Dallas were more frequent. Their lunches and dinners, longer.

Maurice handled what little wedding planning there was himself. On the phone with the minister at Central Christian Church of Dallas, Maurice spoke softly. "Ebby and I want you to marry us. At church on Easter Sunday."

"You want what?" said Dr. Rowand.

"You do that sort of thing, don't you?"

"If you mean marrying people, most certainly I do."

"Well then?"

"I understood the marrying part," Rowand said. "It was the Easter Sunday request that caught me off guard. Easter is a busy day for us around here. We have two services." He paused, "We can do it, I suppose, between services. Say ten o'clock."

"That's fine. We'll keep everything simple. Just a few family members and close friends," Maurice said, and that's what happened. Ebby invited her mother, Lucille, from Kansas and her brother Paul and his family plus a few friends. Maurice's mother, Effie, was there, together with a few long-time church members.

Immediately after the wedding, Ebby and Maurice were off to Chicago for a working vacation—not for Ebby on the speaking circuit, but for Maurice, who had just been elected district governor of the Austin Rotary Club. At the conclusion of the convention, the six hundred district governors of Rotary and their wives boarded the New York Central Railroad, heading for a beautiful antebellum hotel in Lake Placid, New York. There they had more meetings planned and a chance to get acquainted. Maurice had a way about him, a combination of political savvy, and ex-FBI plain-talk that made him a natural at getting to know people. He typically asked a series of quick questions intended to gather interesting facts about new acquaintances. By the end of the three-day meeting, he knew a little about a lot of people and had collected business cards from nearly all the governors.

After the Rotary event, it was time to think honeymoon.

Ebby said, "In the interest of time, why don't we run down to Mexico City for a few days?"

"Fine, Mexico City it is," Maurice said. "As a matter of fact, I recently promised Henry Ramsey, my Austin accountant, and his wife a trip to Mexico City."

"Great. I'll invite my accountant, Bus Burgert and his wife."

"Well, I guess I'd better invite my Beaumont accountant and his wife, Charles and Fern Neuman."

"Is that it?" Ebby asked.

"Now that you mention it, I should probably ask my secretary along, Betty Turner, and her husband, Stan."

"In that case, I'm inviting Mary Frances and her husband, Rufus."

The whole gang rendezvoused at the San Antonio airport. Maurice pulled a few strings and arranged for a mariachi band to serenade the travelers at the foot of the stairway leading into the Boeing 707. The band stood in front of a large banner that read, "The Derring Do Dozen on a Honeymoon." In Mexico City, Maurice had reserved an entire wing of the Alameda Hotel. The area contained a beautiful private lounge, and the staff filled the room with fresh flowers daily. The group congregated in the lounge for breakfast each morning before boarding a bus for sightseeing. One of the excursions took them to Hipódromo de las Americas, Mexico City's horse track. Maurice got the group into the members-only Jockey Club. A reporter from the Mexico City English-language newspaper caught up with the group for an interview and photograph.

The reporter asked Ebby, "Do you always travel with such an entourage?"

"Only on big business deals and honeymoons."

The wedding and honeymoon were, in fact, the least complicated aspect of the couple's getting together. What wasn't so simple was combining their business operations. The process was, according to Maurice, more akin to a merger than a marriage. The merger feature was probably most evident in terms of the living arrangements. The couple effectively had two headquarters—Dallas and Austin—with a satellite office in Beaumont. At the time, Maurice's home was Austin, and he would need to continue living there for Rotary and business purposes. As part of his new duties as district governor, he planned to visit each of the thirty-eight clubs in his district, a plan that required long hours on the road. Ebby, of course, couldn't move to Austin. What had been a long-distance courtship now evolved into a commuter marriage.

Back home, they spent the summer traveling between Dallas, Austin, and Beaumont. This marked the first time in ten years that Ebby had not left the state during a continuous three-month period. At the end of the summer, Maurice began his weekday trips to Rotary clubs in his district, and Ebby traveled to Kentucky and spoke to the Ex-FBI Society of Louisville, of which Maurice was a member. Six weeks later, she was the guest speaker at the monthly meeting of the Chicago Real Estate Board. The trip coincided with the NAREB annual convention held in Chicago, where Ebby was a roundtable participant and was subsequently reelected governor of the National Institute of Farm and Land Brokers.

Just when it seemed there wasn't a venue left in America where Ebby hadn't spoken, she received invitations to talk in Tokyo and Australia. In Tokyo, she spoke at the International Real Estate Federation's annual convention. Three weeks later, after stops in Taipei, Hong Kong, Bangkok, and Singapore, Ebby and Maurice landed in Sydney, Australia.

Before she got down to business, Ebby and Maurice took a quick flight to Canberra, the capital city, where they were hosted for a dinner by Maurice's longtime friend and ambassador to Australia, Ed Clark, grandson of a former Texas governor and a protégé of President Lyndon Johnson. The dinner included the Commissioner of the Australian Federal Police, the equivalent of the FBI. The Commissioner and Maurice traded crime-fighting stories during the evening. Maurice, in prime fashion, saved his rendition of the Weyerhaeuser kidnapping for the final anecdote of the evening.

Back in Sydney, Maurice and Ebby were able to have dinner with members of the Australian Rotary whom they had met the preceding year. They enjoyed seeing the common bond shared by Rotarians around the world. While the real estate industry had its international organization, Rotarians, it seemed, had more than just business to share when they got together. The Australian members and their wives were mildly surprised to learn that Ebby had been invited to speak in Sydney. Her speech, Ebby told them was titled, "The Selling Power of a Woman."

Two days later, Ebby was interviewed on Australia's national television and shortly thereafter spoke to a boisterous crowd of twelve hundred attendees at the Real Estate Institute of Australia. She offered the following advice to the women: "Don't make the mistake of impeding your progress by getting on a soapbox and demanding equal rights. Earn respect by your achievements. Be prepared to give of your time freely, and don't expect to got an office without earning it. Always be feminine. There's nothing worse than the woman who discards her femininity for her career. Don't let your ego show. And remember that success doesn't come overnight. I know from firsthand experience. It's been a long waiting game for me."

Ebby was referring to her recent awards. Prior to leaving for Tokyo, she was elected to the board of the National Association of Real Estate Boards. This was the completion of a trifecta of sorts. Having already been named as the first female Realtor of the Year for her home city of Dallas and what had become her home state of Texas, she now received what was tantamount to Realtor of the Year honors on the national stage.

# CHAPTER ELEVEN
## Moving into the Computer Age

Returning to Texas in May 1966 marked the end of what seemed to Ebby a thirteen-month honeymoon. It was now time to get back to work. The positive effects of the Inter-City Real Estate Referral Service were beginning to show in Richardson, a north Dallas suburb. An increasing number of corporations had chosen Richardson as a relocation destination over downtown Dallas. Of course, the transferred employees wanted to live close to their new offices, and this trend had not gone unnoticed by

Ebby's secretary, Mary Frances Burleson, who tracked company sales statistics. A few months earlier, she had suggested to Ebby that the time might be right to open a new office, and she took the further step of asking to be named manager of the office. Ebby agreed, but with two conditions. First, Mary Frances would need to continue working for Ebby in the mornings for one year, and then build the new office in the afternoons and evenings. Second, Ebby's brother, Paul, would serve as co-manager of the office. The arrangement suited Mary Frances and Paul just fine, and the Richardson office opened a week after Ebby and Maurice returned from Australia.

As was her practice, Ebby didn't micromanage her business. She placed trustworthy people in charge of an office or division. She then let these managers run the business based on their experiences working with Ebby in the corporate office. This strategy allowed her time outside the office where she was at her best, speaking to real estate organizations around the country. After an extended absence from the luncheon and dinner circuit, Ebby hit the road once again. She had accepted several speaking engagements before the upcoming NAREB convention in November. Her first stop was Shreveport for an address entitled "Successful Real Estate Selling Techniques" given to the local real estate board. Later, she appeared at an educational seminar presented by the Ohio Association of Real Estate Boards. What followed were speeches in Dallas; Chicago; Austin; Jackson, Mississippi; Birmingham, Alabama; and Manchester, Connecticut.

Ebby had one additional stop in Kansas City in early November, where the Advertising Club of Kansas City named her Woman of the Year for her efforts devoted to giving women the confidence to succeed in business. She was asked to say a few words, and she gave a new talk, "Real Estate Trends: Influence on the Future," in which she foretold changes in the housing market. A week later Ebby and Maurice attended the NAREB annual convention. Ebby's only official duty was serving as toastmistress for a dinner banquet for the National Institute of Farm and Land Brokers. In subsequent meetings, she was elected and reelected to several boards and appointed to a term as a director of NAREB.

The following year, 1967, Ebby focused her attention on growing her business. By the end of the year, Ebby Halliday Realtors had grown to eighty-three sales agents.

## SURMOUNTING LIFE'S HURDLES

The year nonetheless ended on a tragic note. Maurice's secretary, Betty Turner, lost her husband in a plane crash. Stan Turner worked for the Texas attorney general's office in Austin. He was a pilot and would routinely fly the attorney general to smaller towns that lacked commercial airline service. During a trip in late November, Stan was flying to central Texas to retrieve the attorney general when a storm developed. He set the plane down at a small airport fifty miles short of his destination. He got on the radio and spoke with a pilot who had just landed at Stan's destination airport. The pilot gave Stan an altitude above the storm. The advice proved to be fatal. The following day, a rancher described the scene. A bank of fog had descended rapidly into a valley the previous afternoon and reduced visibility to zero. The search party found the plane on the side of a nearby mountain. There had been no fire; instead, the scene looked as if a bomb had exploded.

Authorities made positive identification when they found a class ring from Texas A&M University, where Stan had played football.

In early 1968, there was tangible evidence that Ebby's network referral strategy was paying dividends. Sales for January, a notoriously slow month in real estate, were the second highest in company history. Many of the sales were directly attributed to the corporate network relocation service. Ebby's firm was way ahead of the competition. Much of the activity was a result of the growth of manufacturing and technology firms in Dallas, which provided military equipment for the Vietnam War.

In January, the North Vietnamese army invaded South Vietnam, with over eighty thousand troops striking at military and civilian command centers throughout the region. The operation was known as the Tet Offensive because it began during the early morning hours of January 31, an important Vietnamese holiday. The objective was to spark a general uprising among South Vietnamese citizens, who would then topple the Saigon government and end the war in a single blow. The offensive was a military disaster for the enemy. However, it stunned American politicians, who believed communist forces were incapable of launching such a massive effort, and it triggered the first real questioning of U.S. war policies.

This was a tumultuous time for the country. A few months later in April, Dr. Martin Luther King, Jr., was assassinated. Dr. King, the leader of the American civil rights movement, had appeared the previous day in Memphis, Tennessee, in support of black sanitation workers on strike for equal pay and better working conditions. King's assassination led to a wave of riots in more than sixly cities nationwide. Two months later, Senator Robert

Kennedy was shot in the Ambassador Hotel in Los Angeles, after winning the California Democratic presidential nomination.

In Chicago, anti-war protesters marched on the Democratic National Convention in August, demanding an end to the Vietnam War. Protesters were outnumbered five-to-one by Chicago police, Army troops, Illinois National Guardsmen, and Secret Service agents. Violence erupted, and the police fought bitterly for control. The confrontation was dubbed the "Battle of Michigan Avenue," where news media recorded the graphic violence— Chicago police clubbing protesters and innocent bystanders, including reporters and doctors offering medical help. The event was an embarrassment to Democratic presidential candidate Vice President Hubert Humphrey, and in the end, Humphrey couldn't overcome the political fallout from the Vietnam War. He lost to former Vice President Richard Nixon in the general election.

## MAKING AMERICA BETTER

In 1969, Ebby got heavily involved with Make America Better, a program formulated by the National Association of Real Estate Boards as a way of attacking inadequate housing for poor families and a host of other problems affecting America's cities. In a speech to the San Antonio Rotary Club, she noted the six points of the Make America Better plan: rehabilitating the slums, educating tenants, removing building restrictions, increasing vocational training, combating crime, and abiding by open housing laws. Ebby appealed to Rotarians to join with eighty-seven thousand real estate personnel across the nation to provide leadership in the Make America Better program, and she served as the organization's ubiquitous spokeswoman for the program throughout the year.

There were bright spots throughout the year. In mid-1969, over one million people crowded the beaches and highways near the Kennedy Space Center, to watch Apollo 11—with its crew of Neil Armstrong, Edwin "Buzz" Aldrin, and Michael Collins—roar into the sunny Florida sky. Four days later, on July 20, Armstrong and Aldrin became the first humans to land on the moon. Like most Americans, Ebby and Maurice watched and listened in awe to the broadcasts from space. Neither of them could have known that Ebby would one day share the stage with one of these three genuine American heroes.

After a two-year hiatus as a featured speaker at the NAREB annual convention, Ebby returned to the podium in San Francisco in November of 1969. She addressed the Women's Council with a talk titled "Ethics: The Right Way and the Wrong Way." She said, "It is our own contact with fellow agents and brokers that often breaches our standards of ethical conduct." As an example, she told the audience that an agent soliciting a new listing might sell himself by knocking the competition. "Oh, you don't want to go with Realtor B. He's all right, but his outfit is too big for your property. I can give your listing more personal attention." Ebby noted that such a comment was a clear violation of the Realtor's Code of Ethics.

She leaned forward on the podium and gazed at the crowd. "I'm reminded of the story of the farmer who raised fine corn. While he won the blue ribbon at every country fair, he always gave his neighbors some of his corn for seed. Someone asked him, 'Aren't you afraid your neighbors will grow better corn and win the prize?' The farmer replied, 'That's what I'm after. I want my neighbors to grow good corn to ensure the quality of my own crop.' If the wind carried pollen from inferior crops it would weaken the quality of the winning farmer's crop." The same principle applies to inter-broker relationships, she told the audience. "A broker who speaks poorly of another broker is planting bad seed, which will eventually blow back into his own field."

## STREAMLINING THE HOME-BUYING PROCESS

After returning from San Francisco, Ebby had one more speaking engagement before closing out the 1960s. The venue was familiar, but the subject matter was not. She spoke to the San Antonio Board of Realtors about the use of computers to streamline the house-hunting process.

NAREB had formed a group of Realtors to look into this newfangled thing called a computer and to report back to the board of directors as to whether there might be some use for the device in the industry. The report was affirmative, and computers revolutionized the real estate industry just as they did almost every other business. Ebby was a member of the evaluation group and therefore became an early adopter of the new technology. She was the first Realtor in Dallas to install computers in her offices.

In fact, the first system installed in each office was not a computer. Even the smallest and slowest computers in the early 1970s lived in big, specially constructed, air-conditioned rooms. What was then referred to as a computer was actually only a teletype machine that was connected by a phone line to a mainframe computer in a remote city. The system was provided by Realtors Computer Service, Inc., and known as the RCS-Realtron. RCS was a Detroit-based company that manually loaded the contents of local Multiple Listing Service databases into its mainframe computers.

Wherever Ebby spoke throughout the year, she managed to introduce the RCS-Realtron to her audience. She enjoyed being at the forefront of new technology, and she was not reluctant to share her newfound knowledge with other brokers. Ebby was simply putting the pollination example into practice. She knew that every broker having the system would accelerate the speed at which all houses could be sold, including her own listings. When Ebby arrived in Chicago for the annual NAREB convention, she devoted a sizeable portion of her "Dynamics of Selling" presentation to the topic of computerized listings. During the convention, she was elected chairman of the National Institute of Real Estate Brokers, the educational affiliate of NAREB, an acknowledgment of her unselfish motivation to raise the level of knowledge within the industry.

Sandwiched into the year was a working vacation for Ebby and Maurice in Dublin, Ireland. There Ebby spoke to the Twenty-First Congress of the International Real Estate Federation. The practice of transferring employees between divisions and between cities wasn't confined to the United States. Brokers from European countries were particularly interested in learning about the network referral system. By now the network had mercifully shortened its name to Inter-City Relocation Service, or ICRS. Representatives from twenty-two countries attended the convention, and after listening to the benefits of the referral service, most agreed there was little reason not to implement ICRS across Europe.

After the meeting in Dublin, the couple traveled to London for a few days of sightseeing. Maurice was anxious to revisit several historic attractions he remembered from his assignment during his FBI days. Ebby had been to London before, but Maurice knew of one destination she hadn't seen, Scotland Yard. The headquarters of the Metropolitan Police Service was referred to as New Scotland Yard or sometimes simply NSY. It housed a museum, commonly known as the Black Museum, not open to the public. However, Maurice still had plenty of friends at NSY who could add him to the guest list. The museum contained an extensive collection of weapons—all of which had been used in murders or serious assaults within London—including shotgun umbrellas and a range of walking stick swords. Also on display were notes allegedly written by Jack the Ripper and a selection of hangman's nooses, including the one used to perform the last hanging execution in the United Kingdom in 1964. Ebby found the tour grimly fascinating.

After the museum, Maurice announced plans for two more stops. Both were along London's Savile Row, famous for its shopping opportunities and traditional men's tailoring establishments. The first stop was at a shoemaker's Maurice had first visited in 1938. He gave the shoemaker his name, and within minutes the man returned with a shoe mold, called a "last," which he had prepared for Maurice over thirty years earlier. With that kind of attention to detail, it was no wonder custom-made shoes hadn't gone out of fashion. At the hatmaker's, he experienced much the same thing. The proprietor located Maurice's hat mold of the same year, and a new hat would soon be on its way to Austin.

To keep Maurice's perfect Rotary attendance intact while traveling, he found the nearest Rotary meeting and attended as a guest. Rotary was similar to fishing from a stocked pond for

Maurice. He would "interview" as many members as possible and collect their business cards to add to his file.

## REPLICATING SUCCESS

The Dublin trip and the ICRS speech were a success. When Ebby returned to Dallas, she had more good news waiting. Her brother, Paul Hanson, had been named regional chairman of ICRS, having served as membership chairman for Texas. With Ebby's public relations work and Paul's operational talent, Ebby Halliday Realtors had led the 452-member ICRS organization in the number of inbound and outbound referrals during the previous two years. Paul would work with the forty-eight member firms in Texas and Louisiana to keep them informed of the best ways to extend ICRS' services to families on the move.

In 1971, Ebby spoke in fifteen cities across the nation. In addition to her repertoire of sales-oriented presentations, she devoted much of her time to outlining the Make America Better program. With the amount of speaking that she had already done on behalf of the program, Ebby had been named co-chairman of Make America Better.

Due to overwhelming success of the RCS-Realtron system, NAREB concluded that a separate entity was needed to handle the growth and administrative operations of the program. To give the business visibility and credibility, the association selected Ebby as the first president. Thereafter, she never missed an opportunity to point out the system's efficiencies and benefits when speaking to local brokers.

Ebby often spoke to all-female audiences on topics like "The Emerging Role of Women in Business" and "Real Estate Is a

Woman's Business." In each, she told a short anecdote drawn from her childhood.

"At ten," she said, "I played baseball with my older brother and his friends. Occasionally, one of the boys asked why I was on the team. I was a girl, after all. To prove myself, I showed that I could hit, run, and catch with the boys, even though I was handicapped by pleated, blue serge bloomers and middy blouses. The experience taught me the ground rules necessary for success in the business world. These are the rules: know your business extra well, ask no special favors, and act like a lady but do business like a man."

In 1971, Ebby Halliday Realtors hit its twenty-sixth consecutive year of sales increases. The steady rise in sales was attributable to many factors: the growing relocation service, repeat business, referrals from previous customers, and the growth of the Richardson office. Six years earlier, Ebby had sent two key staff, Paul and Mary Frances, to open the new office in the suburb of North Dallas. Paul had subsequently returned to the headquarters office to manage the relocation business. The Richardson office kept growing, and soon Ebby sent another key staffer—her very first agent, Mary Lou Muether—to co-manage the office. In retrospect, placing her best people in the field had proven to be one of Ebby's wisest moves. By 1972, the office had grown to twenty-two associates, and it was home to the top-producing agent that year.

## KEEPING BUSY

In 1972, Ebby was elected president of A Beautiful Clean Dallas. She summed up the goal of ABCD by saying, "We want to get every neighborhood, every civic group, every church group, and every community organization involved in the environmental concept." At the same time, Maurice was elected president of the Beautify Texas Council, a nonprofit group aimed at keeping Texas highways clean. Maurice's goal was to eliminate litter by implementing advertising programs and adopt-a-highway initiatives. The couple worked enthusiastically for their causes and brought enhanced visibility to both programs. Ebby quipped to a reporter at the end of an interview that she and Maurice were "just trying to clean up the world."

Later that year Ebby received an invitation to serve on the Defense Department Advisory Committee on Women in the Services. DACOWITS had been established in 1951 by Secretary of Defense George C. Marshall. The committee was composed of civilian women and men appointed by the secretary of defense to provide advice and recommendations on matters relating to recruitment, retention, treatment, employment, and well-being of highly qualified professional women in the armed forces. About the same time, she spoke at the second annual Professional Secretary Seminar held in Dallas. While explaining the role of a working wife, Ebby touched upon some points that she would soon share with the military panel:

> The best way for a woman to preserve her mental health is to have a "split personality." Women are able to work a nine-to-five job and work at home independently of one another. A woman can deal with both segments of her life as a whole person. A woman doesn't lose her identity when she switches from one role to the other. On the other hand, a man very often has only one source of self-respect—his job. If he should lose it, he loses his identity.

You and I are lucky in this way. Our job is important, and we take it seriously, but it isn't our life. The stereotype of a successful man is a decisive, forceful, captain-of industry type. Women, on the other hand, are escaping our stereotyped identity as a helpmate to men. We no longer have to be Edith Bunker. Nor do we have to be Gloria Steinem.

## DOING RIGHT BY THE COMMUNITY

Ebby couldn't say no. She was asked, and accepted, to chair the Small Business Administration Dallas Area Advisory Council. Ebby was the first woman in the organization's history to chair the forty-nine-member group. In explaining to a reporter why she agreed to accept one more responsibility, Ebby said, "The idea of helping people help themselves appeals to me greatly. I believe in free enterprise. I believe in helping people to become tax payers instead of tax eaters."

Busy people always have time for one more project. Maurice was no different from Ebby in this regard. During the year, Maurice was reelected chairman of the board of the prestigious Southwest Research Institute, an independent, nonprofit, applied engineering and physical sciences research and development organization in San Antonio. Southwest Research Institute was the third largest applied science center in the United States. It was later renamed SRI International. Maurice headed the eighteen-member board of directors, which in turn was advised by a one-hundred-fifty-member board of trustees, representing industry, business, science, and academia. It was not a job for a technologically-challenged individual or someone who did not have a good knowledge of intellectual property law. Maurice's FBI background helped with the former and his legal training was beneficial for the latter.

Not to be outdone by his sister and brother-in-law, Paul Hanson was elected president of ICRS in 1973. Paul was the obvious choice, given the award-winning referral results posted by Ebby Halliday Realtors in prior years, as well as his service as regional chairman of ICRS for the past two years. Paul's mission was to expand the membership by finding quality real estate firms in the smaller cities and towns that were not yet represented in ICRS.

## ASKING THE RIGHT QUESTIONS

Even before she became Mrs. Maurice Acers, Ebby was already well known in Houston, Austin, and San Antonio real estate circles. Being married to Maurice only enhanced her stature throughout the state. She had standing invitations to speak to the local real estate boards. In 1973, Ebby's speeches focused on just two themes: empowering women and a broker's responsibility to the community and to the profession. In March, she spoke to the Women's Council of the Houston Real Estate Association. At the conclusion of her remarks, she encouraged the audience to ask themselves the following questions:

Am I doing a good job? Do I merit the trust people have in me? Am I putting anything back into my profession? Am I contributing to my community to make it a better place in which to live, to work, and to do business? The typical member of this group knows, without complaining, that she will have to do better at her profession than any man. She should slip into self-confidence every morning when she slips into her clothes. She should appear at the office or at her appointment each morning expecting to earn her pay. She should leave most of her emotions temporarily in the deep freeze while at work. She should treat the men at work with courtesy and respect and other women the same way. She should be careful and enthusiastic. She should understand her goals and believe she can contribute to her company's achievement. She should never stop learning.

Months later, Ebby addressed the Austin Board of Realtors. Included in her presentation was the following story:

> When I boarded my Southwest Airlines flight this morning in Dallas, a cute, young stewardess wearing hot pants recognized me. The young woman said, "Guess what, Ms. Halliday, I'm in real estate too." Now, I thought to myself, "This is something we don't need. Someone working part-time in real estate. Someone who may or may not be in town when she gets a call from a client." I was ready to ask her how many houses she had sold this year, but before I could do so, she added, "And the pilot is in real estate too." And then I realized this was not only something we didn't need, but something we should discourage. It seemed to me that a pilot's non-flying time could be put to better use staying up to date on aircraft and technical changes. I said to her, "Honey, please tell the pilot if he won't try to sell houses, I won't try to fly airplanes."

Ebby went on to explain that being a real estate professional was more than answering the phone. It was more than driving clients from house to house. It was more than arranging the paperwork. Having another job left little time for civic and community activities, which were essential for success at the job. First, she believed that every professional had an obligation to the community and its people, because the community provided her with her livelihood. Community service was a public relations tool for the individual agent and her firm. She encouraged those in the audience who might see such activities as self-serving to put aside those misgivings long enough to get involved. "Serving on city councils, park boards, zoning boards, committees, and task forces for the YMCA, YWCA, United Fund, and chambers of commerce helps to enhance the image of both the agent and the firm. And this type of service helps the community."

Shortly after she returned from Austin, Ebby Halliday Realtors opened its sixth office in the northwest Dallas suburb of Carrollton. As with the Richardson office, the new office was positioned to take advantage of the job growth in technology-related businesses that were flourishing in North Dallas.

A few months later, the firm opened its seventh office in the northern suburb of Plano. The once-sleepy farming community was transforming itself from cotton fields to rooftops. Plano was large, an area equal to that of Richardson and Carrollton combined, and there would be plenty of room for growth. To insure an efficient launch of the Plano office, Ebby asked Mary Frances Burleson and Mary Lou Muether to manage the newest office. The doors of the Plano office were barely open when the firm became an active sponsor of the community sports association that provided athletic programs for local youngsters. The firm also joined the local chamber of commerce and board of Realtors. The same formula would be repeated each time the firm ventured into a new locale. Ebby's philosophy was to begin giving before she began prospecting.

Later that year, Ebby and Maurice attended the Congress of the International Real Estate Federation convention in Sydney,

Australia. Although Ebby was not scheduled to speak, she and Maurice made it a point to attend because Ebby was a director and Maurice served as the U.S. member of the Professional and Educational Exchange Committee. During August and September, Ebby spoke to various real estate groups in Knoxville, Oklahoma City, Albuquerque, Kansas City, and Minneapolis. The same year, Paul traveled over forty-four thousand miles in his capacity as president of Inter-City Relocation Service. He presided at sixty-one meetings of regional and local chapters. By the end of Paul's one-year term, the name of the organization had evolved once again. The new name was simply RELO.

Ebby was very proud of Paul's work as president of RELO, and she was particularly gratified to see him recognized for his exemplary service by the members of the organization during the annual convention in Washington, D.C. Maurice was also acknowledged at the convention and elected as a director of the International Real Estate Federation. Ebby was, of course, well known to the organization. Anyone in the group whom Maurice had not met during prior board meetings would not escape a quick, pleasant self-introduction and interview from the master fact-finder. Never mind that a fellow director might not speak English. Maurice would offer his business card and always receive one in return, on which he made a few notes for future reference.

As each year drew to a close, Ebby and Maurice had a Christmas tradition of inviting all the associates to drop by their home for lunch during the holidays. To accommodate all one hundred and fifty associates in 1973, the event was spread over three days. In addition to celebrating the season, the firm also celebrated its twenty-seventh consecutive year of record sales.

# CHAPTER TWELVE
## Investing in a Dream and Free Enterprise

In her speeches, Ebby often told the story about how she earned the cash to open her first store, Ebby's Hats, in 1945. As Ebby tells it, by the fall of 1944, she had been working in Dallas at the W.A. Green department store for six years. In that time, she developed a large client list. In the fall, she also developed a sore throat. She visited her doctor, who recommended a tonsillectomy. During the initial visit, a nurse slipped into the examining room and handed the doctor a note.

The doctor glanced at the note. He said to the nurse, "Tell him to buy forty contracts at $20.10."

The nurse disappeared.

Ebby said, "Do you mind my asking what kind of contract costs $20.10?"

"Cotton futures," he said.

Ebby didn't understand cotton futures, but she understood doctors. They were smart. They were rich. The Cotton Exchange Building only three blocks away had well-dressed men coming and going throughout the day. "Doctor," she said, "I've managed to save eleven hundred dollars, and I would like to buy cotton futures with the money."

"Is that so," he said and let the topic drop.

Days later, Ebby made a follow-up visit and asked again about cotton futures.

"I'm a doctor, not a financial advisor."

"A recommendation then."

"To be honest, I don't advise women about finances."

Ebby stared at him.

In answer to her unasked question, he said, "They cry when they lose money."

"I'll take my chances. And I promise not to cry."

"Ebby, it's not only that. Futures are highly leveraged. They're risky, is what I'm saying. You can lose a lot of money very quickly. In fact, most people lose money on futures."

"I've been warned," Ebby said. "So where do we begin?"

Reluctantly, the doctor gave her the name of his broker and told her to set up a trading account. He said he'd let her know when he decided to make his next trade. Weeks later, the doctor called Ebby at the store to say he was ready to buy more cotton contracts. "I'm recommending you risk no more than $200 on this trade. Remember, you will need to have money in your account if the trade starts to move against you. And don't forget to place the stop loss order we talked about."

"Thank you, doctor. I'll keep that in mind," she said.

Ebby called her broker and bought $1,000 worth of cotton futures. To cover her bet, she set a stop loss, which protected a part of her money if the price of cotton dropped by as little as a few hundredths of a cent per pound, something that could happen in the blink of an eye. If the price dropped, she'd lose about half of her investment.

After placing her trade, she made a point of passing the Cotton Exchange Building each day and checking the price of cotton. By the end of the first day, the price had risen slightly. For every hundredth of a cent the price increased, the value of Ebby's contracts rose $200. Ebby watched as the price continued to climb. After almost three months, the price of cotton had risen about six-tenths of a cent per pound, and her futures contracts were now worth about $12,000.

Ebby closed out the contracts and put the money in her pocket. After seventeen years in retail, Ebby was convinced she could run her own hat boutique, and now she had the money to do just that. After moving the money to her checking account, she gave notice to Consolidated Millinery's regional manager. She told him of her plans to open a hat shop in a renovated house on the northern edge of downtown. She had expected the worst, but the manager's response surprised her. He asked her to carry the Consolidated line of merchandise in her new store.

## STAYING THE COURSE

Not all business challenges could be navigated so smoothly. Thirty years later, in 1974, the nation faced a host of pressing issues—Watergate, an OPEC oil embargo, rising oil prices at home, inflation, and others. The result was higher mortgage rates and slower home sales. However, a curious psychology was at work. Ebby spoke to a group at the Metropolitan Real Estate Board of St. Louis and explained the real estate market this way: "Most people feel rising home values will offset higher interest costs." Put another way, now was the time to buy before inflation pushed home prices even higher. This pressure to buy kept home sales moving.

In May, Ebby gave a commencement address titled "What Now in Today's World" at the University of the Ozarks. To keep her company, Ebby invited a friend along. After her speech, Ebby and her friend drove to the small town of Leslie, Arkansas, where Ebby grew up. Ebby arranged for a childhood acquaintance to drive the two around the town and point out the sights. On a back road, the driver pointed to a beautifully painted little house. She said, "That's where your Uncle Dorsey lives. He's away in Washington right now."

Ebby's friend asked, "Oh, is he in Congress?"

Ebby laughed. "No. He's picking apples."

Shortly thereafter, she was off to Chicago for the annual meeting of the National Association of Real Estate Boards. The organization had undergone a name change. It was now the National Association of Realtors, or simply NAR. After Chicago, Ebby and Maurice hopped a plane for Madrid, Spain, for the annual congress of the International Real Estate Federation. Their appearance marked the first time a husband and wife served as directors of the organization.

Ebby had a busy schedule. She spoke in Fort Worth, in Orlando, and in Kansas City with her brother Paul at the national RELO convention. A week later in August, she spoke at the University of Dallas Graduate School of Management about how best to manage a growing real estate company.

By August, Watergate reached a boiling point. Eight days earlier, the United States Supreme Court had ruled that President Nixon must hand over tape recordings of conversations made inside the White House. He complied, and the tapes revealed that Nixon had attempted to cover up the Watergate hotel break-in. Nixon resigned his presidency on August 8, 1974, and Vice President Gerald Ford was soon sworn in as the thirty-eigth president. Two months later, President Ford spoke at the NAR convention in Las Vegas. He announced a government program to stimulate home sales. Ford told the crowd, "The real solution will not be provided by the government. The victories must and will be won in the market place." The speech was generally viewed as a tacit admission that the United States was moving toward a recession.

In spite of bleak national economic forecasts, Ebby Halliday Realtors was doing well. Home sales were up 15 percent over the previous year, and Ebby opened her eighth office at the intersection of Preston Road and Beltline Road. If the eighth office was a statement, then the ninth location was visionary. The ninth office opened the following year on the mall level of a newly completed sixteen-story office tower. The new location was the most modern of her offices and underscored her commitment to the city and her own business.

Late that year, she received good news. In a letter to Ebby in her role as president of A Beautiful Clean Dallas, Dallas Mayor Wes Wise informed her that the city had been selected to receive the National Special Merit award given by the Keep America Beautiful organization. His letter thanked Ebby for her support: "Contributions such as these make our city a more pleasant place to live. The priceless gifts of time and talent given by the many participating organizations have helped Dallas to achieve a very coveted position. I can't think of a more positive way to reinvest in our communities than to take a personal interest in the cleanup, restoration, and beautification of our surroundings. Please accept my personal congratulations and appreciation for a job well done. Your success reflects favorably on the entire city."

And that wasn't all. Good news came in waves. What followed was a letter from the White House.

## VISITING THE WHITE HOUSE

A mailgram from the White House got right to the point.

*Ebby Halliday*
*Dallas, Texas*
*On Wednesday, February 5, 1975, I will be hosting a group of business executives to discuss the economy. I would like to invite you to join me, Frank Zarb, Russell Train, and other administration spokesmen for a free flowing discussion and exchange of ideas. We are especially interested in your ideas and recommendations in dealing with business and the economy. The meeting will begin at 9:45 a.m. in the Roosevelt Room of the White House and will be followed by a luncheon in the White House executive dining room,*

*hosted by Gary Seevers of the Council of Economic Advisors. We will adjourn by 1:30 p.m. Please R.S.V.P. and contact me with any questions.*

*The White House*
*Washington, D.C. 20500*
*William J. Baroody Jr.*
*Assistant to the President*

Ebby was, of course, honored to be invited but was skeptical that only a three-hour and forty-five-minute meeting could produce any useful results. The timing was unfortunate. She was scheduled the day before to speak at a zoning meeting in the afternoon on behalf of a client. So long as the zoning board stayed on schedule, Ebby could state her case and catch a late plane to Washington. For some, serving on a municipal board was a stepping-stone to higher office. As a result, hidden agendas could emerge unexpectedly. Ebby's case was delayed because of a squabble among zoning board members. By the time she left city hall, she had to rush to the airport to catch the last flight out of Dallas.

During the White House meeting with administration officials and some twenty other participants, Ebby offered suggestions for boosting the economy. Her primary concern was turning around the anti-business, anti-profit, and anti–free enterprise sentiment mounting in Washington. She began by suggesting that antitrust laws should apply to labor unions as well as corporations. She noted that labor unions were monopolistic by nature and there was little logic for exempting unions from antitrust laws. She believed that base pay increases, for example, were appropriate only when production increased, and that such regulations should apply equally to every labor organization in the nation. Higher pay without increased production would only feed inflation and make the nation uncompetitive in world markets. Ebby concluded by saying, "It is important to encourage the spark of the capitalistic system, a system that makes our economy better than others throughout the world."

By the time she returned to Dallas that evening, she had been awake for thirty-six hours straight. After catching up on her sleep, Ebby discovered she had been named "Distinguished Salesman of Dallas" by the Sales and Marketing Executives of Dallas in recognition of outstanding business and civic leadership. In making the presentation later, the president of the organization explained that Ebby had specifically asked that the award retain the "Salesman" designation, although she was the first woman to achieve the honor in the club's twenty-seven-year history.

In subsequent speeches, Ebby returned to familiar ground— her alarm over a growing bias against the free enterprise system. She had become a spontaneous surrogate for the Ford administration. Her trip to Washington had influenced her in subtle ways. She realized that many of the other White House meeting participants were popular speakers within their industries. By mobilizing opinion makers from the private sector, the Ford administration had in effect intensified its battle against inflation by getting private enterprise to do what the government couldn't all by itself, which was espouse the benefits of free enterprise, create jobs, and fund growth.

Ebby spoke at the Dallas Chapter of Executive Secretaries and told the group that success was a matter of priorities. She suggested that to be successful, the following guidelines would prove helpful.

- First, prepare for a chosen career or profession. The days of hope and luck are gone. Now that marrying at an older age, or not marrying at all, is no longer frowned upon, and now that planning a family is common practice, every young woman should prepare for a career—something she enjoys and could rely on for a living.
- Second, communicate well. Learn to speak well and dress in businesslike attire that reinforces your professional message.
- Third, practice the art of getting along with people. Brinkmanship seldom wins friends.
- And fourth, learn how to sell. A good saleswoman was always in demand, no matter the profession.

She added, "Success is the result of making choices; preparing for that choice; getting along with people; developing an innate desire to do well; fostering an inner belief that what you do has value; and nurturing the expectation of equal pay for equal work and an equal chance of promotion."

## PROMOTING FREE ENTEPRISE

In subsequent speeches to real estate agents and salespeople, Ebby stressed the need for selling the free enterprise system while selling their usual products. The American people needed to be reminded that making a profit was not an unworthy pursuit. The free enterprise system had produced the high standard of living the nation enjoyed, and all four million salespeople in the United States owed their livelihood to this system. For her local talks, Ebby combined her motivational message with an optimistic review of the region. She referred to the new DFW Airport and how the project had led to an unprecedented expansion in international business coming to the area. She reminded groups that it was possible that the influx of businesses to Dallas might help the region to avoid a recession altogether.

In October, Ebby traveled to Nashville and Cleveland. Her presentations were designed to dispel the gloom of high interest rates and high inflation. She emphasized that women have come a long way in many fields and certainly in real estate. Women were active in all aspects of real estate—residential sales, commercial sales, managing, and appraising. One of the more satisfying aspects of residential sales was the absence of sex discrimination with regard to pay. "In an eat-what-you-kill environment," Ebby told audiences, "the landscape is relatively flat." She explained how she got her start in the millinery business and that the rules for selling hats were just as applicable to selling real estate. The customer was always right. Winning an argument never won a sale. Always do what you promise, and do it when you said you would. She cautioned listeners to remember that clients were impressed by what they saw when they looked at you, what they heard when you spoke, and what they felt in your presence.

Shortly after the Cleveland speech, Ebby flew to San Francisco for the annual NAR convention where she served as vice chairman for the week. She was honored during the convention and appointed the first woman president of Omega Tau Rho, the honorary society of NAR.

By the end of 1975, sales for Ebby Halliday Realtors were up 17 percent from the previous year. The year also marked the company's thirtieth anniversary and the thirtieth year of consecutive continuous growth in sales. When asked how the company achieved its stellar sales record, Ebby was ready with her answer. "First, our growth is connected to the growth of Dallas and the surrounding cities we serve. Second, we have great management talent, highly trained professional sales associates, and a company philosophy promoting good service. Third, the firm has maintained continuous growth in facilities and technology. We now have nine well-located neighborhood offices. And fourth, we have our exclusive RELO program, which assists corporate transferees when buying a home in a new city. Even with thirty-year mortgages averaging 9 percent and an inflation rate to match, Ebby Halliday Realtors participated in 2,340 transactions last year."

Ebby's free enterprise remarks resonated with her audiences. In a speech to the Dallas Advertising League in early 1976, she said, "Our young people must be taught the dangers of a constantly increasing bureaucratic system, of a system that takes from productive citizens and gives to able-bodied, non-productive citizens. No nation can approach or match our free enterprise system. That doesn't mean we can perpetuate our system without working to preserve it, without fighting for it. We must be on the lookout for anti–free enterprise forces. These forces include organized labor, welfare groups, and liberal politicians who seek to discredit our capitalistic system."

Ebby's business continued to grow. The RELO program paid big dividends. During the year, Associates Corporation of North America moved its headquarters to Dallas, and Ebby and her team helped one hundred and fifty employees find new homes.

By the end of the year, Ebby Halliday Realtors home sales were up 42 percent over the previous year.

## COOKING IN PARIS

To celebrate the record-breaking year, Ebby and Maurice traveled to Paris for a working vacation. First, the two attended the annual meeting of the International Real Estate Federation. While there, Ebby was elected vice president of the residential committee, and Maurice was elected vice president of the professional and education exchange committee, making them the first couple to serve at the same time as officers of FIABCI. Next, they took a few extra days in Paris for an excursion to Lyon. It was the third largest city in the country and located about four hours southeast of Paris between two of France's best known wine-growing regions— Beaujolais to the North, and Côtes du Rhône to the South. Lyon had a reputation as the French capital of cooking, which was precisely the reason Maurice planned the trip.

Maurice loved to cook. He had recently reduced his residences from three to two and would now have more time for his favorite pastime. He often joked, "Ebby likes my cooking, and I like her selection of pots and pans." As a member of Chaine des Rotisseurs, an international gastronomic society, Maurice loved to discover and try new recipes. The Lyon excursion gave the couple an opportunity to experience nouvelle cuisine, a specialty of one of the finest chefs of the twentieth century, Paul Bocuse.

When their train pulled into the Lyon station, Ebby and Maurice were met by a driver who took them a short distance outside the city to the village of Collonges-au-Mont-d'Or, Paul Bocuse's hometown. Bocuse met them at the door of his restaurant, l'Auberge du Pont de Collonges. Inside, the fireplace was ablaze and helped to warm the crisp December air. The restaurant was designed in a French country motif, oil paintings on the walls, elegant and informal china, and simple silver patterns.

Ebby and Maurice were special guests, and Chef Bocuse treated them like royalty, standing formally beside their table, summoning his sous chef and station chefs to the dining room and introducing them to the American couple. Next, the headwaiter explained the specials of the day. Ebby selected one of Chef Bocuse's signature dishes, Black Truffle Soup Élysée. Following the soup, the waiter brought a selection of twenty cheeses. The soup, cheese, and a glass of wine put Ebby and Maurice into a cozy mood. By the time they finished with coffee three hours later, the couple agreed the experience had been much more than they anticipated.

L'Auberge du Pont de Collonges wasn't the last stop on their gastronomic getaway. After their flight landed in New York, Maurice and Ebby made their way downtown to Luchow's, a ninety-four-year-old German restaurant and an institution in New York City. Luchow's occupied the entire block between 13th and 14th Streets. Its seven public dining rooms and two private dining rooms made it the city's largest and most historic restaurant. Maurice loved German food, and the evening was made even more festive by an eye-catching, twenty-four-foot Christmas tree resting in one corner of the main dining room. Dinner at Luchow's became a Christmas tradition for Ebby and Maurice.

## MAKING DO IN HARD TIMES

The year 1977 was one the most challenging economic periods in American history. The country was mired in stagflation, inflation, and public apathy over continuous price increases. The economy found itself in a vicious cycle of rising prices, rising wages trying to keep pace, and prices shooting even higher. Labor contracts included cost-of-living clauses. Social Security payouts increased. Inflation stood at 5 percent, while mortgage rates hovered around 9 percent for a thirty-year loan, high by recent historical standards.

Despite the poor economic conditions, Ebby Halliday Realtors had a record-breaking year. Home sales were up 27 percent. The RELO corporate relocation program was going strong. Only a handful of firms received referrals on a consistent basis, and Ebby was by far the leading beneficiary of this prized business—prized because many of the relocating executives were on the "transfer track." She knew that today's buyer was tomorrow's seller. In a slow market, and without a strong referral base, many marginal real estate firms closed up shop.

As the market contracted, Ebby Halliday Realtors picked up market share and in the process hired experienced agents looking for work. The silver lining was that it was a good time to be in real estate. Inflation didn't hurt the business as much as many other professions. With the rise in housing costs outpacing the rate of inflation, an agent's income was automatically adjusted upward whenever a sale closed.

The following year, interest rates climbed again, and, defying logic, the Dallas housing market also expanded. Ebby Halliday Realtors grew to meet the demand. Ebby opened three more offices in 1978, bringing the total to sixteen. Doubling the number of offices in three years required additional administrative personnel. To accommodate the new staff, Ebby and Maurice purchased a pair of duplexes and transformed the structures into a single dazzling office with a glass atrium connecting the two buildings. The result of all this growth: Ebby Halliday Realtors posted more record-breaking sales results.

# CHAPTER THIRTEEN
## Training for Tough Times

The newly converted atrium building became Ebby Halliday Realtors' new headquarters. In addition to the inspiring two-story atrium, the conference room had been equipped with the latest training equipment: a remote-controlled rear-screen projection television for slides and motion pictures and a sound system. The new location also served as the training facility. The training program had been formalized into Ebby School, a two-week agenda that introduced new agents to the company history, customer service, mortgages, taxes, real estate exchanges, neighborhoods, and the legal aspects of selling real estate.

Maurice Acers was the company's chairman and general counsel. He also taught Ebby School's sessions on the legal and regulatory issues in real estate. He was an enthusiastic and humorous lecturer. He stood at the podium entertaining the recruits with tales of outlandish real estate escapades by prospects, clients, and business competitors. But the highlight of Ebby School was always Ebby's presentation. She explained the rewards of a career in real estate and what it took to become successful. She mentioned all the things she had preached on her speaking tour for the past thirty years: enthusiasm, commitment, community involvement, an organized home life, communication skills, and appropriate dress.

As the company improved its recruiting and training processes, Ebby opened two additional offices in 1979, a bold move in the face of rising mortgage rates and untamable inflation. Gasoline prices hit a dollar per gallon. Mortgage rates hovered at 12 percent, and the rate of inflation topped 13 percent. The new chairman of the Federal Reserve Board, Paul Volcker, took great pains to stifle inflation by driving up short-term interest rates to the point that most businesses couldn't afford to borrow and effectively shutting down the money supply. Despite the restrictive monetary policies, Ebby Halliday Realtors finished with another record year.

## REWARDING EXCELLENCE

In 1980, Ebby and eight other Realtors were the first recipients of the National Association of Realtors Distinguished Service Award. The award was the first of its kind for the 750,000-member trade organization, given for "exceptionally meritorious service to the profession and the public." Ebby was the only woman and the only Texan to receive the award.

A few weeks later, Maurice received the International Real Estate Federation Medal of Honor. He had served three consecutive terms as chairman of the professional and educational exchange committee, during which the scope of the program had expanded for students and professionals studying real estate on a worldwide basis. Maurice had been instrumental in establishing an international exchange program which allowed hours accumulated in foreign study to be applied to a college degree. To facilitate the program, he lobbied American universities to offer scholarships for foreign students studying in America. And to set an example, he established the Ebby Halliday Scholarship Fund to support students studying real estate at Southern Methodist University.

In June, Ebby was awarded Woman of the Year by the Dallas Chapter of the Women's Council of Realtors. This was the same organization Ebby had launched twenty-six years earlier as its president. Months later, she received the Outstanding Woman of Achievement in Real Estate in the United States award from the International Organization of Women Executives.

Ebby Halliday Realtors, as an organization, received several awards at the Mid-Winter RELO convention in San Diego. For the third consecutive year, the firm took first place in the advertising competition with a television commercial and billboard theme, which proclaimed, "Ebby Is Your Friend." The company also took first place among twelve hundred member firms in two categories in the RELO competition: combined referral sales and total outbound referrals.

A reporter for *The Wall Street Journal* interviewed Ebby and produced a flattering front-page story. On April 3, 1980, the *Journal* described Ebby Halliday Realtors' corporate relocation program, how the program had evolved from helping individuals find a new home to helping entire companies relocate to Dallas. According to the article, the company was instrumental in smoothing the way for organizations like Dresser Industries, Associates Corporation of North America, Lennox Industries, Celanese Chemical, American Airlines, and Diamond Shamrock to resettle in the Southwest. Revenue from the company's relocation services accounted for 40 percent of total revenue in 1979. In the story, Ebby noted that with mortgage rates at 15 percent, companies were now making "mortgage-rate-differential" payments to compensate transferees for the higher interest rates on their new homes.

The story in *The Wall Street Journal* led to more speaking invitations. The extra demand sparked an idea: why not use surrogate speakers to handle requests Ebby couldn't fulfill herself? No need to pass up an opportunity to have the firm's name recognized at key events. Ebby selected two of her top people to go out and speak on the company's behalf. Mary Frances Burleson, executive vice president and general sales manager, and June Feltman, former manager of the Preston Center office. Both were familiar with public speaking, and both had conducted countless sales meetings. Ebby recommended that both women begin attending Toastmasters International to polish their speaking skills prior to hitting the speaking circuit.

## RECRUITING AN EBBY TEAM

Ebby had an ulterior motive for cutting back her speaking engagements. She and Maurice decided to open two more offices in 1980. The new offices brought the total to twenty. Ebby focused on recruiting the staff for an Ebby-caliber team. She spoke at several universities in the area, combining her recruiting message with her inspirational outlook.

At the closing session of a student-led free enterprise symposium, she told students, "Never has the world offered so much to young people. The opportunities to succeed are all around you. Learning the principles of free enterprise will be a marvelous beginning. Our capitalistic system, even with its faults, is the best system in the world. And you have an opportunity and privilege to make it better." She slipped in a recruiting pitch by telling the group that college graduates could go into real estate and begin making a substantial income. "The choice for young people embarking upon their careers has never been so great, especially for women. This is the best time in the world to be a woman and the perfect time for women to succeed in business."

Ebby didn't confine her speeches to real estate. During a talk to the Home & Apartment Builders of Metropolitan Dallas that summer, she told builders that the Carter administration had mishandled the economy. "In spite of all that's gone on in Washington, we've been lucky here. Construction in the Dallas area almost boggles the mind. Nonetheless, our businesses stand to lose momentum if we have four more years of the same. The present administration's mishandling of the economy has hit everybody, but Realtors and builders have born the brunt of the problem with sky-high interest rates." She noted that national home sales were beginning to pick up, but if the Democrats in power were not replaced, a home construction slump could happen again. "I say let's throw the rascals out of office," she told the audience. "The Carter administration has done our country a great disservice. We now have a chance with Ronald Reagan and George Bush to set this nation back on track."

## PASSING THE TORCH

After a few warm-up speaking appearances, Mary Frances was ready for the big leagues. In January of 1981, she was asked to speak to the Royal Institute of Chartered Surveyors in London, England. Her topics were "Better Negotiating Techniques" and "Increase Your Listings." Ebby described the invitation to a local reporter by saying, "We are very proud to have Mrs. Burleson represent us in England. It is an honor to appear before this professional British real estate organization." Ebby described Mary Frances as "one of the top professional women in the industry."

While Mary Frances was in England, America was in a recession. President Reagan was forced to admit as much in October of 1981. Several key industries, including housing, steel, and automobiles, experienced dramatic downturns. By September of 1982, however, chairman of the Federal Reserve Board, Paul Volcker, had policies in place that appeared to break the back of inflation, pulling the rate down to 5 percent and in the process leaving twelve million people unemployed.

Meanwhile in the Sunbelt, the oil-patch and related industries remained reasonably healthy. The reason was the new oil crisis. Oil prices rose from fourteen dollars a barrel in 1978 to thirty-five dollars a barrel in 1981. At the higher price, domestic oil exploration in the Southwest became profitable once again. With new exploration came jobs in oil drilling, equipment sales, oil field services, and supporting commercial financial services. Dallas got its share of the activity and with it an increase in demand for commercial real estate. The oil boom touched off a commercial building boom in Dallas like none the city had ever experienced. Oil companies and oil-related partnerships needed office space, and bankers couldn't loan money fast enough to keep large-scale contractors happy and construction moving along. All this activity was taking place in the face of the Federal Reserve's policies to ward off inflation by keeping interest rates high. Commercial lenders ignored the Fed and passed the cost of high-interest loans on to anyone with a plausible rationale for repayment.

New construction meant new jobs. And new jobs attracted workers from the Northeast. An influx of home buyers was good for the residential real estate market. The problem was that unlike commercial banks, home mortgage lenders scrutinized every loan application. With mortgage rates in the 15 percent to 17 percent range, many would-be homeowners couldn't make the mortgage payment and therefore couldn't afford to buy a home. This situation created a demand for apartment rentals, which in turn, spurred additional commercial development. While the rest of the nation was economically anemic, the Southwest was experiencing spectacular growth.

Remarkably, the same period produced three more record-setting years for Ebby Halliday Realtors. By summer of 1983, inflation had been tamed, having fallen from a rate of almost 15 percent at the beginning of 1980 to 2.5 percent in July. With mortgage rates falling to pre-1979 levels, pent-up demand for housing blossomed. To celebrate the return of lower interest rates, Hank Fulmer, an employee in the relocation division, composed new lyrics to the tune of "Happy Days Are Here Again." As a kid, Ebby had learned to play the ukulele and so could manage the three chords needed for the melody. She dusted off her 1929 uke, and after a few days practice, debuted her new act at a meeting of the North Dallas Multiple Listing Service. She opened by saying, "You know, I really can't play the ukulele or sing, but it helps to have a shtick; everybody needs a shtick."

*Interest Rates Are Down Again*
(To the tune of "Happy Days Are Here Again")

> *Happy days are here again,*
> *Interest rates are down again,*
> *Mortgagees have fixed-rate loans again,*
> *Happy days are here again.*
>
> *Builders' starts are here again,*
> *Hammers fly and roofers grin,*
> *Home buyers rush to buy again,*
> *Happy days are here again.*
>
> *And even if closings are slow,*
> *They're bound to be up, we know—*
> *So, all of us can smile again,*
> *We'll all be sure of jobs again,*
> *We know that salesmanship will always win,*
> *Happy days are here again.*

Ebby received a wild round of applause. A seventy-two-year-old rock star had been born.

# EMERGING FROM RECESSION

By the summer of 1983, the entire nation had emerged from recession. Unemployment dropped. Interest rates plunged. Corporate profits rose. To keep up with demand, Ebby Halliday Realtors needed more sales agents, and more agents required a larger training facility. The company had outgrown its corporate headquarters in only five years. After more than thirty years in Preston Center, Ebby and Maurice decided to move the company's headquarters to a centralized location. The new location six miles to the north offered more space, improved meeting facilities, and ample parking. Ebby's signature location at the corner of Northwest Highway and Preston Road would remain a branch office. Ebby Halliday Realtors home sales in 1983 jumped a whopping 58 percent over the previous year, a result of 9,416 transactions for the year.

Almost one year later, in November of 1984, the rate of unemployment declined even further, and President Reagan carried forty-nine of fifty states in the presidential election. Ebby had campaigned for the Republican ticket throughout the year. Her message was that capitalism was the greatest economic system ever devised. Reagan's reelection was a shining symbol that free enterprise would survive.

In early December, Ebby attended a career counseling day for high school seniors. She shared her advice with students about opportunities in real estate. Sprinkled throughout her message was a healthy dose of the importance of a market economy. She offered the following guidance:

Salesmanship is the bedrock of the real estate business. The man or woman working on straight commission is a true representative of the free enterprise system. There is no assurance of a set income and at the same time no limit to what you can earn. If you're willing to make selling your top priority, give up evenings and weekends, make learning a habit, and put service to the public first, you can make it in this business. Real estate is a wonderful career, and I encourage you to look into it. The Constitution of the United States guarantees your right to own the land under your feet, to sell, and to develop it. Our economic system provides the incentives to build your fortunes using real property. Whether you want to become an investor, a real estate agent, or a home owner, real estate is the basis of the American Dream.

As Ebby's speeches began to include more politics, Maurice was evaluating his own political views. The outcome was a major shift in his political thought, and he converted from a Democrat to a Republican. As Maurice told Ebby, "I didn't leave the Democrat party; the Democrat party left me." In spite of the optimistic economic outlook, two sets of economic storms began to appear.

## SURVIVING IN A BUST ECONOMY

The looming economic storms had names—the "Oil Bust of 1986" and the "Tax Reform Act of 1986." The oil bust devastated real estate values. The tax reform act removed tax shelters for real estate investments and in doing so crushed the real estate industry, the savings and loan industry, and major commercial banking in Texas. Either event alone would have been enough to cause a recession. Together, they were ruinous.

Of the two, the oil bust caught everyone by surprise. In the run-up of oil prices in the early 1980s, oil producers had gotten used to higher oil prices and higher profits. However, by November 1985, the price of oil had slipped from forty dollars to twenty-eight dollars a barrel. To make matters worse, a pricing ploy devised by the twelve countries that make up OPEC to drive high-cost producers out of the market backfired and caused prices to tumble to twelve dollars a barrel by February 1986. Prices dropped to ten dollars a barrel by midsummer. A drop in oil prices was good news for consumers and bad news for Texas. Practically overnight, almost every Texas oil producer, oil-related company, and oil investor, including banks and savings and loan organizations, was wiped out.

Oil companies fired employees. Exploration stopped. New commercial office construction ground to a halt. Residential housing projects collapsed, and with the collapse, home prices tumbled. Many homeowners simply walked away from their mortgages because the value of their homes was far less than the loan balance. Overnight, the Texas economy had become a joke. A popular gag went like this: "Did you hear about the new model Mercedes is building for Texas real estate developers? It has no seats and no steering wheel. It's for guys who have lost their rear end and don't know which way to turn."

The Tax Reform Act of 1986 was equally destructive. The tax bill cut the top tax rate from 50 percent to 28 percent and closed a host of long-standing tax loopholes. Among the perceived loopholes were the tax benefits of owning real estate. Minimizing allowable tax deductions and making the tax rate the same for capital gains and ordinary income evaporated the market for commercial real estate syndications. Stripped of the tax benefits, there was little reason to own improved real estate—the return on investment for owning office buildings and rental property was simply too speculative to justify the risk.

Even in the midst of such economic calamity, Ebby Halliday Realtors posted a record-breaking year for 1985 and in doing so celebrated forty years of continuous sales increases. There was no way to extend the record to forty-one. By August 1986, Ebby's home sales were down 10 percent from the preceding year. By the end of the year, the decline had worsened to 20 percent. The good news, according to Ebby, was that opportunities to make money still existed. Prices were lower, and interest rates were down.

Ebby believed the economic slump would last another eighteen months. How long exactly depended on upcoming amendments to the tax bill and the price of oil. The problem for large real estate firms like Ebby's was in covering fixed expenses—corporate salaries and office rent—until sales picked back up. The revenue to cover expenses came from commissions earned on home sales. Even a slight dip in sales could affect the paper-thin margin between a profit and loss.

No amount of hard work and determination would overcome the overwhelming tide of economic disruption. The company suffered another year of declining sales in 1987. Things could have been worse. That they weren't was credited to first-time homeowners who bought homes at depressed prices and lower interest rates. Much of this sales activity was at the low end of the market. The mid- and upper-end markets were essentially dead. Home sellers could not sell their homes for enough to pay off the underlying mortgage, which left them little or no money to get into a new home.

Within this crumbling market, sales associates began to flee for other occupations. More than 1,000 residential agents in the Dallas Metroplex quit the business in the late 1980s. Ebby was able to hold onto her top talent because she had built an extensive infrastructure of technology, training, advertising, administrative support, legal review, financing options, corporate relocation services, and other functions that allowed her agents to focus solely on selling houses.

## LEASING AND MANAGEMENT SERVICES

Ebby Halliday Realtors had another source of revenue to help survive the bad economic times ahead. Ten years earlier, Maurice had established a separate leasing and management services division. This small group of dedicated staff had low overhead and stellar profits. In the past, when interest rates fell and home sales rose, the leasing business leveled off. However, as interest rates climbed and sales declined, the leasing staff worked overtime to handle all the new listings. By the mid-1980s, the division was the largest leasing operation in Dallas. During the downturn, profits from the leasing division helped to cover the sales division expenses for office rents and corporate staff.

Mary and Uly Vlamides were two of Maurice's earliest recruits to the leasing department. The couple had owned three steak houses in Dallas for several years, but by 1978 the seven-day-a-week grind had taken its toll. Maurice learned of their plan to sell the restaurants and asked if he might speak with them about working with him. During an interview, he warned them that the leasing business was hard work. Mary said, "Mr. Acers, we've been in the restaurant business. Leasing houses will be a piece of cake!" And apparently it would be. The couple is now regarded as the best in the business at leasing and managing residential real estate properties in the Dallas area.

Ebby Halliday Realtors ended the year with total dollar sales down another 5 percent, but with total transactions up a few percent over the previous year. A recovery was slowly materializing.

## CHANGING OF THE GUARD

Ebby had named her brother Paul Hanson president of the company, and he had taken her admonition to heart about becoming involved with the community. Paul had joined a range of civic organizations and served as an officer in several. He had, in fact, followed in Ebby's footsteps in being elected a director of the North Dallas Chamber of Commerce. By early 1989, however, Paul believed it was time to step down as president of the company and let Mary Frances Burleson assume day-to-day responsibility for running the company.

Paul first met Mary Frances shortly after she joined the company as Ebby's young assistant in 1958. He watched as she learned the real estate business and enjoyed the time they spent together as co-managers of the Richardson branch office in 1966. By 1979, Mary Frances had been promoted to vice president and general manager of sales. More recently, Mary Frances had become a spokesperson for the company and routinely spoke to the local media about the Dallas market. With over thirty years of experience in the real estate business, she was well-suited for the role of president.

Promoting Mary Frances was a win-win-win. Paul was able to reduce his hours, Mary Frances was given the recognition she deserved, and Ebby was able to begin a succession plan for management of her company.

The fact that Mary Frances was coming into the job on the heels of the worst economic decline in forty-five years was bad luck and a great opportunity. She likened Ebby to the Pied Piper in her ability to attract and retain people. While reminiscing about her career, Mary Frances admitted that the real estate business had seemed chaotic at first. She soon found that spontaneity to unique situations that arose every day was much more interesting than a daily routine. Her initial duties were to organize the chaos and help agents sell more homes. Thirty-one years later, she was doing more of the same.

Mary Frances found herself at the right place at the right time. By the end of her first year as president, the market showed signs of a turnaround. The company ended the year with a 13 percent increase in sales and an 11 percent increase in sales transactions.

## BANKING BACKLASH

Even after a foreclosure, many Dallas-area banks couldn't sell the homes in their inventory. This was common in the late 1980s because most of the properties for sale at auction were worth less than the loan balance, interest, and fees. A good example of the fall of Dallas-based banking was the demise of two of the area's largest banks, Republic National Bank and First National Bank. The banks' loan portfolios were hit hard by real estate devaluations.

After dumping undervalued property assets from their portfolios, the banks still didn't have the reserves to stay afloat. In a desperate attempt to salvage these once mighty institutions, the two companies agreed to merge in 1987 to form First Republic

Bank Corporation. The experiment was short-lived, however, and the Federal Deposit Insurance Corporation stepped in and took over the merged bank in what was then the largest bank failure in United States history, requiring over $3 billion to cover member deposits. By 1989, an out-of-state bank had swept into town and acquired the bank. The scene would be repeated many times by other out-of-state banks until there were no major Dallas-based financial institutions left standing.

In one sense, the turnover in bank ownership proved beneficial to the housing market beginning in 1990. Competition among competing banks for customers was keen and fueled a resurgence in the housing market. Dallas was suddenly a sellers' market. Sales of existing homes in June set a new record for a single month. By year-end, total sales for the firm were up 15 percent, and the number of transactions jumped 20 percent.

With two years of double-digit growth under her belt, Mary Frances was off to a blazing start in her role as president. While 1990 had been a banner year, continuing this growth would prove difficult. Economic conditions throughout the United States were still depressed. In August, President of Iraq, Saddam Hussein ordered troops to invade Kuwait and capture its oil fields. President George H. W. Bush spent the next five months amassing military troops and supplies in Saudi Arabia and assembling a coalition of nations to counter the Iraqi offensive. On January 17, 1991, U.S.-led coalition forces entered Iraq in order to return Kuwait to the control of the Emir of Kuwait.

At home, the country slipped into a recession, with little consensus as to the cause. From July 1990 through March 1991, the U.S. economy showed the slowest growth rate since the

Great Depression. The general gloom sent consumer confidence tumbling, and home sales in Dallas slipped by more than 20 percent during the first five months of the year.

A quick resolution of the Gulf War spurred the housing market, and by the end of the year, sales for Ebby Halliday Realtors showed modest gains. The real estate recovery caught fire in 1992. A small uptick in interest rates coupled with rising prices early in the year stimulated sales. Once again, Mary Frances found herself in the right place at the right time. In the interim, she had been elected president of the Greater Dallas Association of Realtors. When asked by a reporter for her opinion of the market, she responded: "I've been telling everybody things were getting better, and this is it. Traffic is good, open houses are good, buyer confidence is up, and people are out looking for homes." In fact, Mary Frances' outlook was dead-on. Company results for 1992 topped the previous year and established new records for sales and transactions. The company finally surpassed its previous all-time record set in 1985.

# CHAPTER FOURTEEN
## Making Every Day Count:
## Treasuring the Moments

In the spring of 1992, Ebby, Maurice, and a small group of friends attended a graduation exercise at a local university, where a longtime friend received an honorary doctorate degree. After the commencement, the group walked to the reception a few hundred yards away. Halfway there, Maurice became short of breath and grabbed a nearby tree and held tight until the symptoms subsided. He had first experienced shortness of breath in 1983, when he was seventy-six. Tests at that time revealed he was suffering from idiopathic pulmonary fibrosis—scarring of the lungs—or IPF, a progressive interstitial lung disease that limits the lung's ability to transfer oxygen to the bloodstream. He learned the causes of such a disease were widespread—cigarette smoking, pollutants, certain diseases, radiation treatments, and some medications.

Maurice had been a cigarette smoker for much of his life. He finally kicked the habit in his early fifties. Once he quit, he became one of those intolerant ex-smokers, the kind who didn't hesitate to let bystanders know their smoke bothered him. He even handed smokers a business card. It said, "The family who smokes together, croaks together."

At the time of his diagnosis, there was no cure and no effective treatments. The average survival time was two to four years. Maurice decided not to reveal his condition until he had no other choice. By the spring of 1992, however, he had no other choice. Each year Ebby and Maurice returned to Austin in August. The trip coincided with Maurice's birthday but was actually an excuse to keep up with old cronies from the FBI and his state government buddies in Austin. He and Ebby held an annual party at the Headliners Club. Festivities began in the late afternoon and continued into the night long after sunset.

By the time the two attended the party in 1992, Maurice had been outfitted with a portable oxygen system. Near the end of the evening, he made his way to the microphone and announced this would be the last birthday celebration in Austin until he turned ninety-five. Until then, he told the group, he hoped to see everyone in Dallas each year for the annual celebration.

Years earlier, he wrote a spur-of-the-moment note that described his philosophy. "In this world, a person is what he means to another. What he can do for another. Otherwise, he is just a collection of minerals and liquids. Soon to disappear, to reenter life's never-ending nitrogen cycle."

Even after Maurice began using the oxygen system, the decline was gradual. He would enjoy several additional months of fairly normal, albeit somewhat limited, activity. In fact, there would be one more trip to Austin to see more friends, but this time it was Ebby making the plans. A group of Maurice's Rotarian friends in Austin asked Ebby if Maurice was up to another trip to Austin. Yes, she told them, his spirits were good, and she thought that he would like to do that. However, they arranged it to be a surprise party. The ruse was that Ebby had to speak to a meeting of the Keep Texas Beautiful chapter in Austin during the spring of 1993, and she asked Maurice to come along. The noon "meeting" was scheduled for a local Mexican restaurant. But when Ebby and Maurice walked in, a Mexican fiesta erupted to welcome him back to Austin one more time. The surprise worked, Ebby knew, because he would have never worn a three-piece suit if he thought he was going to a party that day.

Shortly after the Austin trip, Maurice became increasingly dependent on the oxygen machine. He stopped going to the office, instead dressing each morning and sitting in the sunroom, reading mail and talking on the phone. In the afternoon, Betty Turner came to the house with the mail from the office, and Maurice dictated return correspondence. By late July, his condition had deteriorated. He was admitted to the hospital where Ebby stayed around the clock in an adjoining room. A few days later, Betty got a call from Maurice asking her to come to his hospital room. When she arrived, he dictated a series of letters to close friends. Betty said later, "It was very, very sad for me. But Maurice wasn't sad at all. Writing the letters was something he wanted and something he enjoyed."

The day after he had dictated the letters, the doctor suggested to Ebby this was a good time to notify next-of-kin. The following morning, the hospital suite filled with visitors pleased to find Maurice awake and alert. He turned to Ebby and asked her to call Dr. E.C. Rowand, their longtime minister and the man who had married them twenty-eight years earlier. Betty located Dr. Rowand, and when the minister finally arrived, the two old friends spoke for a few moments. Betty Turner left for the office and an hour later received a call. Maurice Acers had passed away.

Maurice's death was the saddest moment of Ebby's eighty-one years. Memories and emotions swept through her mind, emotions she hadn't allowed herself to anticipate until the moment arrived. The only man she ever trusted implicitly was gone.

# CHAPTER FIFTEEN
## Partnering with People You Value

Since Maurice's death in 1993, Ebby has continued to live a rich life and grow her business by focusing on her company's core mission: serve the client, serve the communities, and serve the industry itself. Sharing her ideas, partnering with people she values, encouraging women to get involved, giving back to the community, keeping pace with technology, supporting her sales team, and recognizing accomplishments are all part of an ongoing message: improve your life by improving the lives of those around you.

Maurice Acers was Ebby's husband and lifelong friend. He was the man who bought her the ukulele she entertains audiences with today. With little prodding, Ebby can recall the Honeymoon Express, an image of Maurice, Ebby, and ten others being greeted by a mariachi band at the foot of a Braniff 707 jet in 1965. To hear Ebby tell it, her marriage was filled with travel and adventure.

When Ebby and Maurice married, he became Chairman of the Board of Ebby Halliday Realtors and general counsel, while still maintaining an office and home in Austin. At the same time, Ebby was named Chairman of the Board of Acers Investment Company. The two embarked on a twenty-seven-year odyssey of work, personal growth, and volunteering. Maurice left this world a better place and touched many lives.

In 1999, Southern Methodist University asked to archive Maurice's papers. Ebby donated a number of his documents to the university. They are held in the DeGolyer Library in its rare book and manuscript collections. She also donated papers of her own to the Archives of Women of the Southwest.

In addition to Maurice, one of Ebby's most cherished partners is her company president Mary Frances Burleson. On Maurice's death, Ebby became chairman of the board, and Mary Frances succeeded Ebby as president and CEO. Many of Ebby's responsibilities now revolve around maintaining the contacts and influence she and Maurice cultivated, while Mary Frances runs the day-to-day business operations.

Mary Frances joined Ebby Halliday Realtors in 1958, some fifty years ago, as a temporary office worker, a Kelly Girl. Since then, she has promoted the same "service first" attitude that propelled Ebby in her personal and professional life. In 1999, both

Ebby and Mary Frances were named to the list of "Top 300 Power Brokers" by *National Relocation & Real Estate Magazine*. In an interview for the magazine, Mary Frances said, "When the public likes and trusts a company and its people, they do business with that company. That is the reason we have remained successful for so many years."

Ebby and Mary Frances have nurtured their relationship throughout the years. That positive bond, as much as any other factor, has helped attract new support staff and sales agents to a company known for hiring family, and if not family, then friends who stay with the company long enough to be considered family.

The company isn't solely about family or friendship, but also about identifying a strategic advantage, dedicating resources, and implementing processes to exploit the advantage. One of the things that distinguished Ebby Halliday Realtors from its competitors was the company's early focus on relocation services under the direction of Ebby's brother, Paul Hanson, who passed away in 2007. Paul's philosophy was simple: give better service to home buyers and sellers, give better service to the people in direct contact with buyers and sellers—the company's own sales force. In the same magazine article, Mary Frances said, "Better service is just a matter of enhancing, nurturing, and keeping an open mind. And always, above all else, stay on the cutting edge of technologies that will help enhance our service offerings."

Another helpful strategy is to offer consistent service and benefits. Whether a client is moving around the corner or to another state, Ebby and Mary Frances encourage sales staff to give one hundred percent to every transaction. To make sure that happens, the company invests heavily in training and education and has one of the most well-respected training programs in the real estate industry.

There is no question that Ebby and Mary Frances are a team. The two have worked together cooperatively for half a century in pursuit of the same goals: to serve the client, serve the communities, and serve the industry. In 2003, Ebby and Mary Frances were presented a Kim Dawson Attitude Award to honor individuals whose personalities and accomplishments enhance the lives of those around them.

## GROWING THROUGH ACQUISITIONS

Perhaps it has been Ebby's reluctance to sell out to larger firms or otherwise compromise her independence that has caused her to avoid actively looking for other companies to acquire. Two notable exceptions have occurred in the past fifteen years, however, that have proven to be spectacularly successful. In 1995, Ebby acquired Ellen Terry Realtors, a firm specializing in high-end properties in the Dallas area. The company continues to operate under its own name but under the Ebby Halliday umbrella. Likewise, in 2007, the company acquired the Prudential Real Estate office of Dave Perry-Miller & Associates in the Dallas area. Dave Perry-Miller & Associates specializes in the Park Cities area with an assortment of exclusive listings. Like Ellen Terry Realtors, Dave Perry-Miller & Associates continues to operate under its own brand but as a member of the Ebby Halliday organization. Another acquisition opportunity arose at approximately the same time, and Ebby decided to take advantage of it, also. But unlike the two previous transactions, the agents for the firm of Adleta Fine Properties were dispersed among the Ellen Terry offices and the Dave Perry-Miller offices.

The acquisitions provided the impetus behind a move to re-brand the Ebby corporate environment. Each of the three sales organizations continues to retain its own identity: Ebby Halliday Realtors, Ellen Terry Realtors, and Dave Perry-Miller & Associates. However, the corporate office now operates under the banner of *Ebby Halliday Companies*, which just proves that businesses, like families, can thrive by adoption.

Before she makes a move to acquire a company, Ebby consults with her long-time CFO and CPA, Ron Burgert, who performs the due diligence on proposed deals. Ebby Halliday Realtors has had only two CFOs—Ron and his father, R.F. "Bus" Burgert. And just to keep it all in the family, Leonora Burgert worked in the accounting department for her husband and then her son from 1947 to 2005. Ebby credits the Burgerts with keeping the company solvent for sixty-three years.

## INSPIRING WOMEN

On several occasions, Ebby has joked with audiences, "I've never traded on being a female. I worked like a dog and acted like a lady." At the heart of this humorous quip is the bedrock of Ebby's commitment to herself and to all women. By example, Ebby gave women hope throughout her career. She encouraged women to enter the job market at a time in the 1940s, '50s, and '60s when divorce, being single, or worse—being a single working mother—was scorned.

Ebby offered women who wanted to work outside the home an opportunity to engage in business. She educated women and gave them a way to make a very good living. Not surprisingly, her employees and associates, 80 percent female by the way, tend to be highly motivated and fiercely loyal, with more than seventy having been with the company for over twenty-five years.

Through her position as Chairman of the Board of Ebby Halliday Realtors, her speaking activities, her work in community organizations, and her board memberships, Ebby has done much to break down barriers for women in business. She was the first female president of the North Dallas Chamber of Commerce, the first woman named Texas Realtor of the Year, the first female chair of the Real Estate Brokerage Council, the first Woman of the Year of the Dallas Real Estate Board, and the first woman recipient of the Sales and Marketing Executives of Dallas' Distinguished Salesman Award.

Dallas is home to women-owned businesses, large and small. They've faced challenges, but they have also prospered. A climate of equal opportunity for women has flourished in Dallas and in Texas as a whole. Even in such a positive environment, operating a business or becoming a successful businesswoman has not been easy.

Throughout her career, Ebby has received thousands of letters thanking her for her encouragement. One letter was sent in January 2003 by Dorothy Killebrew, a widow at thirty-six and sole support for six children.

*Dear Ebby,*

*This letter is to express my appreciation for your most generous help. I went back to school in the eighties, receiving a BA in 1985, an MEd in 1993, and a PhD in 2002. I teach sociology, specializing in marriage and family. In my classes, when we reach the topic of welfare versus women in the workplace, I often tell my own story. I*

*urge women to complete their education because when times get
tough they may not have a friend like Ebby Halliday.*

*This is my story.*

*When my husband died in 1963, I became the sole support of
six children. I was thirty-eight at the time and had no job skills. My
neighbor, an Ebby Halliday Realtors sales associate, worried about
my ability to provide for my children. She encouraged me to come
to her office and meet with you. You were polite and asked me to
sit. We talked briefly and you said, "I like you, Mrs. Killebrew. I want
you to work for me. I'll teach you myself. I haven't trained anyone in
five years, but I want to train you. Watch me when I talk with clients
and others by phone and in person. When you have questions,
speak directly to me. Ask me anything. I'll always help you."*

*Ebby, those kind words of yours were, to me, a sunrise and a
new beginning. The values that you modeled were more important
than the fundamentals of real estate. You taught me humanity in
the workplace, kindness, and empathy. I was encouraged by the
soft odges of the business world that responded to humanness. I
saw for myself that compassion and fulfillmont were core business
ideals and the outcome of a job well done. You modeled humor,
and when events conspired against me, I soon learned to take the
day's happenings with a grain of salt.*

*One evening at dusk, I came home clutching a contract. I
called you and said, "Oh Ebby, the buyers signed the contract."*

*"What about the sellers?" you asked.*

*"I haven't presented it to them yet."*

*"Don't ever let the sun go down on a contract."*

*"But Ebby, the sun is already down."*

*"But it's shining somewhere."*

*I took your words to heart. Your sense of humor highlighted the role perseverance plays in the business world. I truly loved working under your guidance. I was always happy and proud to say I was an associate of Ebby Halliday. You made a real difference in my life and the lives of my children. May God bless you always and keep you in His tender mercy. You will always be in my heart.*

*Sincerely,*
*Dorothy Killebrew*

Within the same envelope, Dorothy's son had included a letter of his own.

*Dear Mrs. Halliday Acers,*

*I have been writing this letter since 1963. I think it is time to complete it and mail it. I can't remember how many times you and Mr. Acers have helped my mother, brothers, and me. Looking back over a thirty-nine-year history, you made the single greatest positive impact on my mother's life and my life. You appeared as an angel of God at a time of grief and loss in our lives, and gave personalized training to Mother.*

*I think of the parable, "Give a man a fish and he will have one meal. Teach the man to fish and he will eat for a lifetime." What you gave my family was so much more than a meal or charitable donation. You helped my mother face life, to succeed in raising six children, and all without the help of a husband.*

*Your counsel helped her grow as a parent, in wisdom, and in virtue. It is because of your unselfish gifts that Mother has pursued her dream and earned her PhD in Sociology from the University of North Texas.*

*Today I work for the Texas Department of Human Services. I am a Medical Eligibility Specialist and test applications for Nursing Home Benefits. This last Christmas, one of the cards I received from a client had a handwritten note inside. It said, "You are an angel. Where do you hide your wings?" My inspiration comes from my mother, you, and Maurice. Each of you taught me life lessons by example. Today I am so grateful for my life, and I wanted to thank those who have influenced me. I only wish I had thanked Maurice before he died. Somehow, I suspect he was pleased enough just to help, as I feel you are.*

*Mrs. Halliday Acers, thank you for being there in 1963 and throughout the years for my mother Dorothy Killebrew, my brothers, and me.*

*Sincerely,*
*David R. Killebrew*

## GIVING BACK

In 1992, Ebby handed over 49 percent of her company to her employees. She created an employee stock ownership plan, and her employees now own nearly half the company. Upon her demise, the remaining 51 percent goes into the same trust. Such a gesture has created a corporate culture with committed owner-like employees. When asked about the employee stock ownership plan, Ebby said she didn't want to sell the company. She didn't want to franchise it. What she wanted was to leave shares to the people who helped develop and run Ebby Halliday Realtors.

For years now, Ebby has believed that philanthropy means more than giving money or company stock. It means giving time.

Give money, and you give from your pocketbook. Give time, and you give from your soul, she says. Ebby is a genuine philanthropist, no matter how you measure it. Her generosity of time and money is legendary. Her contributions demonstrated her deep commitment to the city she has helped shape.

In the January 2001 issue of *Real Estate Business*, in an article titled "Texas Powerhouse," Ed Fjordbak, then-president of Communities Foundation of Texas, noted, "Ebby encompasses all aspects of philanthropy. From a financial perspective and with her most precious commodity, her time. I have often wondered how she finds the time to work on so many projects, serve on so many boards, and create so many things for the benefit of the community, and at the same time, run one of the leading real estate concerns in the country. I don't know how she does it, but she does. And she does it exceptionally well and graciously. She is a consummate professional and businesswoman, a true leader of this community and a very generous philanthropist. We are privileged to have her as chairman of CFT's Advisory Council. She is an invaluable link to the business and professional worlds."

To Ebby's way of thinking, giving back to the community isn't merely a privilege, but an obligation. She encourages all sales associates to contribute whatever time they can—raising funds, volunteering time, or serving others. Start small if you must, but start, she says. Ebby started small. One of her first sponsorships was supporting a Little League baseball team for young boys in North Texas. Her slogan at the time was: "Big on little folks."

She is the first to admit that it is sometimes difficult to distinguish between doing good for one's company and doing good for one's community. In Ebby's opinion, business and charity work are in tandem. She believes in giving from the heart and increasing visibility in the community to produce success that allows more giving. The cycle benefits the individual, the company, and the community.

Volunteering, working for a local community organization, helping at a hospital, a service club, or a political or environmental action committee, no matter the source of your inspiration, is probably a good thing. Ebby and others like her serve as a model for massive action and minimal excuses. Ebby's philanthropy has inspired many to provide a continuum of care and contributions for the neighborhoods in which they live and the industries and organizations in which they participate. When Ebby is asked to serve on a board, chair the fundraiser, lead an advisory council, or host other time-consuming projects, she says yes.

## MOVING INTO THE TWENTY-FIRST CENTURY

In 2003, Ebby Halliday Realtors unveiled a new marketing approach that included a new Web site, logo, advertising brochures, and freshly spruced-up yard signs, a staple of the real estate business. The new marketing look included TV, radio, newspaper, and online ads geared toward the public announcement of its new look. The advertising showcased a new ad on one of the most visible billboards in Dallas, near the intersection of I-35 and I-635. The giant billboard said simply, "Ebby.com, the best address in real estate."

Today, imagining a time when computers, cell phones, text messaging, and Web sites weren't common tools of the real estate trade can be difficult. Ebby Halliday Realtors has created a state-of-the-art presence. Using the latest technology, the company offers information and services to clients and sales associates alike. Ebby.com provides clients online access to search for properties, locate leasing information, tap into relocation services, and find mortgage financing, office locations, career information, and company history. Additionally, while relying partially on computer-based training, Ebby has created one of the best training courses in the business.

Ebby and Mary Frances have assembled a team of tech-savvy executives who have been at the forefront of developing applications, using emerging technologies. They have identified key trends affecting the business and, when no off-the-shelf programs existed, created their own in-house solutions. One of the trends is that of Baby Boomers searching for scaled-down housing and willing to do much of the legwork by looking for property online. Generation Xers, on the other hand, are on the move, transferring jobs, searching out unique life experiences with more flexibility. They want loft or condo living and short-term leases. Xers are taking advantage of Ebby.com's property search, relocation services, leasing options, online mortgage shopping, and insurance services.

In keeping with the changing times, RELO changed its identity in 2005 to Leading Real Estate Companies of the World (Leading RE), to better describe the scope of the organization that Ebby helped to found more than forty years earlier. Her company is one of three firms in the Dallas area that are members of Leading RE today. While many home buyers use the Web, e-mail, cell phones, text messaging and other technologies to search for a home, others can't even turn on a computer. Ebby Halliday Realtors is adapting to customers rather than squeezing them into a single mold.

Technology, all by itself, warns Mary Frances, isn't the enchanted forest. Technology is a useful tool that helps meet customers' needs—searching for a home, clicking through Web pages of communities in more than a dozen North Texas counties, surveying the neighborhood, looking at photos, and getting answers to questions on topics ranging from home inspections to appraisal valuations. Online tools enable clients to get the information they need quickly and efficiently.

But Web access to information is only part of the home-buying equation. What customers say they want and what it is they really want can't be reconciled while sitting in front of a computer. Buyers need to get out and walk through properties. They need to see and feel the neighborhoods. They need to shop local markets and town centers. Home buyers need to build a relationship with a flesh-and-blood sales associate. They need to talk and share and, when they find a property, negotiate. Technology—whether Web access or computer-based training or more efficient relationship management tools for sales associates or enhanced management support—is only a tool to facilitate the home-buying process.

## SUPPORTING THE PEOPLE WHO SUPPORT THE CUSTOMERS

The quality of any real estate office can be measured by the quality of the sales force. If this group of independent contractors stays happy, so will the customers. Both Ebby and Mary Frances have worked hard to develop new and innovative ways to support the sales team. The company revamped its sales support tools in 2008. The new Business Development and Sales Support program includes a wide range of tools to help more associates sell more property and ensure better customer satisfaction.

Many of the new support tools are accessed online via the company's intranet. Tools include a My Listings Dashboard that links agents to a service center where they can easily manage their inventory. The dashboard allows associates to create and send full-color property progress reports. These progress reports are typically sent to clients and include the associate's photo and contact information. The report breaks down elements in the selling process—number of property showings, ads placed, number of views—displayed in different colors for easy reading. The dashboard allows associates to add listings and to complete MLS input sheets in minutes. To showcase properties, agents are encouraged to upload high-resolution photos of any size, which will be automatically resized in the process, and store the photos online for use in future marketing promotions.

Another sales support tool is the Ebby Ink Shop, a new online print program that allows associates to generate, proof, and order graphics from an intuitive interface. Marketing materials are generated in a fraction of the time it takes to order from outside vendors. All orders sent to the print shop are guaranteed for next day delivery.

The sales team has access to a new customized buyer/seller packet creation tool. An associate can create highly tailored presentation materials by simply checking a box for key data that apply to a specific client or area. Key data might include general area information, local sites, schools, local employers, property taxes, steps in the buying process, and others. Clients receive only the detailed information they want.

The intranet includes an Associate Flyer Program for sales associates to print flyers at home from a library of templates. Flyers can be used for open house announcements, invitations to special luncheons, and reduced-price announcements. The Web site has many other associate-centric tools, including property open-house indicators, open-house reminder E-cards, a "New Listing" star for ten days to help attract attention and boost traffic, and a tool to create a client record, with an inventory of thumbnail photos of properties to be shown to a prospective buyer.

The new business development program includes agreements with prestigious online magazines to feature the entire MLS inventory. Additional online presence includes a strategic partnership with HGTV.com (to promote residential listings), LandWatch.com and Resortscape.com (to promote farm, ranch, and resort listings), and LuxuryRealEstate.com (to promote listings priced at $600,000 and above).

## RECOGNIZING ACCOMPLISHMENT AND SERVICE

Throughout her career, Ebby has been recognized with many awards. Her long list of accomplishments was the result of hard work and a willingness to serve others. She received the Distinguished Service Award from the National Association of Realtors early in her career, the Medal of Honor from the International Real Estate Federation, the Lifetime Real Estate Achievement Award from Texas A&M, and the Most Influential Woman in Business honors from the Fort Worth Business Press.

Ebby was the first inductee into the Hall of Leaders by the Real Estate Brokerage Manager Council of the NAR. The Dallas

Chapter of the Texas Association of Business honored Ebby with the Distinguished Business Leader Award, which put her in elite company. The St. Paul Medical Center Foundation honored Ebby and Maurice by allocating $2 million on behalf of Maurice Acers to build a new Emergency and Chest Pain Center.

Awards and formal recognition are the rewards of leaders and companies who transform intangibles like values, ethics, and ideals into practical outcomes like jobs, revenue growth, and profits. Ebby applied her heartfelt principles in ways that were meaningful to herself, her employees, and her community. When Maurice died in 1993, Ebby was eighty-two years old. Since then, her commitment to community activities and the resulting recognition has grown. Her accomplishments are numerous. In 2000, *Realtor Magazine* selected Ebby as one of twenty-five most influential people in the industry. She received the Servant Leader Award from the Volunteer Center of Dallas County, the Texas Association of Realtors Lifetime Achievement Award from the Real Estate Center at Texas A&M University, and the Real Estate Lifetime Achievement Award presented by the center.

Ebby was the recipient of the prestigious Linz Award given to a resident of Dallas County whose civic and humanitarian efforts benefit the City of Dallas. She received the Medal of Courage Award from the 12th Annual Dallas Blue Foundation, the Girls Champion Award from Girls, Inc., and the Murphy Award for Lifetime Achievement from the Murphy Enterprise Center at the University of North Texas.

One of her most cherished awards, however, was the Horatio Alger Award given by the Horatio Alger Association of Distinguished Americans. In 2004, Steve Durham, chairman of

Americas Strategic Alliances, helped recommend Ebby Halliday for the Horatio Alger Award, an honor Steve's father, Charles W. Durham, received in 2002. Steve first met Ebby in 1995, while attending a board of directors meeting for the Thanks-Giving Square Foundation, an organization dedicated to supporting the concept of giving thanks as a universal, human value.

The Thanks-Giving Square board was a diverse collection of members who in many ways mirrored the foundation's theme of tolerance for interreligious and multicultural attitudes. Nonetheless, disputes about the direction of the foundation's projects were routine. A skirmish arose, and Steve, new to Dallas and the board at the time, stepped in to negotiate a truce. He soon found his impartiality caving to the logic and charm of one of the combatants, Ebby Halliday. It would be a few years later before Steve and Ebby made the connection between Omaha, Steve's hometown, and Ebby. The eighteen-year-old daughter, Margre, of one of Ebby's Omaha customers, later married Charles Durham, and the couple had four children, the oldest of whom was Steve.

As disputes go, this one was relatively minor, and the ruckus soon subsided. Yet based on that first encounter, nine years later, Steve helped recommend Ebby for the Horatio Alger Award. The Horatio Alger Association is dedicated to the simple belief that hard work, honesty, and determination can conquer all obstacles. Ebby was the perfect candidate. She'd started with nothing and by 2004 had a company with twenty-five offices, twelve hundred agents selling 17,500 homes a year, and annual sales of $3.8 billion.

Steve met with Ebby and Randall Graham, the company's marketing director, for breakfast and explained the qualifying process. Ebby, in her modest way, tried to defer. No, she didn't deserve it; there were plenty of other worthy candidates; maybe in a few years—all the excuses that Steve had expected.

"Humor me, Ebby," Steve said.

"There are other people more deserving than me."

"Why don't we let the evaluation committee decide?"

"Fair enough," she said.

The applications and biographical material were prepared and sent to the association headquarters within days. All that was left were the letters of recommendation. Before it was all over, the chairman of the nomination committee, Walter Scott, Jr., received an armful of recommendations by well-known leaders: Ross Perot, Norman Brinker, Edwin L. Cox, Ray Hunt, Tom Harken, William P. Clements, Jr., Carol Keeton Strayhorn, and Nancy Dedman. Nancy added a postscript to her recommendation. "P.S. Since Ebby is already ninety-three years old, let's not dilly-dally on her nomination."

Ebby received her Horatio Alger Award in April of 2005 at a ceremony in Washington, D.C., and she was in good company. Of the other nine recipients, two were from her own city—then 7-Eleven Inc. CEO James Keyes and then Southwest Airlines President Colleen Barrett. And almost thirty-six years after Ebby and the rest of the world watched grainy pictures from outer space, Buzz Aldrin—the second man to set foot on the moon—was also honored that evening.

Ebby began her acceptance speech by telling the young students who were receiving scholarships that the freedom and free enterprise system of the United States gives everyone an opportunity to succeed. And that it had certainly given her one.

After noting that many of her employees and associates had been with her for more than twenty-five years—and forty-seven in the case of Mary Frances—she advised the scholars to never give up and to never, never retire.

Other examples of long tenure who were present in the audience that evening included Betty Turner, who had begun as Maurice's secretary in 1961 and was now one of Ebby's two secretaries. Ebby's other secretary, Anne Anderson, had been with the company since 1981. Ron Burgert, who had been with the company for twenty-eight years, was also in attendance.

Next, Ebby mentioned that she had been encouraged to give an anecdote which depicted her age. She began, "I'd really forgotten that I was ninety-four until something happened recently. One of my associates called and wanted my help with a fabulous house in Highland Park that was not yet on the market, but that she thought might be getting ready to be listed. She knew that I knew the owners, their parents, and their grandparents. So, I made the call, and the housekeeper answered and said that the lady of the house was not in. I asked her if she would please have her call Ebby Halliday when she returned. She said, 'Well, who should she ask for?' and I said 'Ebby Halliday,' to which she replied, 'Lord, is she still alive?'"

After the laughter died down, Ebby noted that she was still going strong, and with the help of Mr. Greenspan who (from his post as president of the Federal Reserve System) had driven interest rates down to levels unseen in forty-five years), the company had just completed its best year ever. She noted how much she valued being a citizen of this wonderful country. She pointed out that the Horatio Alger Association was giving the young scholars an opportunity for an education, which she had not been able to get very much of, and that such an education would be a wonderful asset to their lives. "And besides that, it will make you good taxpayers," she quipped.

Once again, Ebby drew a round of applause, but it was minimal compared to her closing remark, which followed one last thank you to the Horatio Alger Association. She looked at the audience, paused with impeccable timing, smiled, and delivered the showstopper line of the evening, "I am so pleased to be alive."

Few human beings reach their nineties. Fewer still receive an award at that age and are able to attend a ceremony bestowing the honor. And daresay there is only a handful who can provide the entertainment for such an event—at the age of ninety-seven. But such was the case in May of 2008 at the Midyear Legislative Meetings and Expo of the National Association of Realtors held in Washington, D.C. In celebration of the one-hundredth anniversary of the formation of the NAR, the president of the association, Dick Gaylord, chose Ebby to serve as the honorary chair of the Centennial Black Tie Dinner. Many in the crowd of thirty-five hundred that evening probably had the same reaction as the Highland Park housekeeper, but there was little doubt as to her status when she finished her updated rendition of "Happy Days Are Here Again" while accompanying herself on the ukulele. Ebby updated some of the lyrics to reflect the changes brought on by technological advancements.

*Interest Rates Are Down Again*
*Version 2.0*
*(To the tune of "Happy Days Are Here Again")*

*Happy days are here again*
*Interest rates are down again*
*It's a sellers' market once again*
*Happy days are here again.*

*That's the way it used to be*
*A simpler world for you and me*
*But now we have "Tech-nol-o-gee"*
*It's different now, it's plain to see.*

*There's the Internet and E-mail, too*
*The World Wide Web's no longer new*
*You fax me and I'll fax you*
*These are wondrous times—it's true.*

*Our good old ways will never do*
*A firm handshake between me and you*
*Now it's mediators and lawyers, too*
*We may be sued before we're through.*

*But through it all we've stood real tall*
*We've learned new ways . . . we're on the ball.*
*We can be proud—one and all*
*And RELO days are here again.*

To mark its one-hundredth anniversary, The NAR published a beautiful commemorative volume—*100 Years in Celebration of the American Dream*—containing the history of the association and photographs and short biographies of fourteen of the most influential individuals in the history of the association. Headlined as "Real Estate Giants," the narratives were sprinkled throughout the book and paid tribute to the leading pioneers and innovators of the residential real estate industry over the past one hundred years. Of the 294 pages of material, six were devoted to Ebby. Only one other individual was accorded as much space. In addition, several other photographs of Ebby at various stages of her career were displayed throughout the book to denote the advent of new trends in the industry over the years.

Although she has received countless awards during her career—including numerous "firsts"—the recognition bestowed by the National Association of Realtors during the one-hundredth anniversary celebration was in many ways the culmination of a magnificent career and a lifetime of achievement. But this is not to say that Ebby has retired, nor will she. As she has said so often when asked for advice on living a long, healthy life: "Don't smoke; don't drink alcohol, and never retire!"

## Looking toward the Next Fifty Years

E bby Halliday Realtors has enjoyed phenomenal success. In the last fifteen years, sales transactions have grown by 168 percent and sales volume by 375 percent from $1.3 billion to $4.9 billion. The number of sales associates grew from 805 to 1,559, support staff doubled to 220, and the company continues to grow. This raises the question: just how does a company with such a history of growth continue to expand? The answer is by focusing on customers, employees, and the community. Put another way, Ebby, Mary Frances, and the senior management team are constantly striving to answer these questions: What do our customers want? What do our associates and employees want? How can we best serve our community?

Ebby, now ninety-seven, has watched the real estate industry change from individual associates selling one house at a time to real estate organizations with massive resources influencing the way home buyers relocate, evaluate, finance, and insure new home purchases. In the early years, computers, online services, shared databases like the Multiple Listing Service, and national networks like RELO, were nonexistent. Today, Ebby Halliday Realtors is on the cutting edge of technology, computer-based training, virtual tours, e-Business, marketing and branding, specialized real estate services for seniors, mortgage services, insurance services, and corporate real estate services. Information technology has dramatically affected the way home buyers make buying decisions, and Ebby Halliday Realtors has made adapting to these changes a strategic priority.

In 2007, the company's information technology teams focused on two critical projects: the company's intranet, and implementing a new accounting system. The intranet included a new and easy way to interface new tools—property search, graphics ordering system, video conferencing, buyer tour reports and property progress reports, photo uploader, automated MLS input sheet, a shared bulletin board—and other programs designed to support sales associates who then provide better service to home buyers. The new accounting system offers better transaction tracking, reorganized income and expense accounts, specialized data entry modules, search and filter data, and other features that allow managers to track and analyze key performance indicators.

In 2009, technology continues to be a company focus with a revamped Web presence incorporating individual property and agent Web sites, a home page specifically formatted and optimized for mobile phones, increased videos, customer-centric reporting tools, blogging and other social media programs.

The company's basis for growth is its sales force, associate training, key services, supporting services, marketing presence, locations, and information technology infrastructure. With all of these elements in place, the Ebby Halliday organization is poised for even greater growth.

In addition to traditional residential real estate services, the company has created supporting business divisions to bolster its bottom line. Ebby Halliday Corporate Real Estate Services closed $858 million in sales in 2007. The Corporate Business Development division worked with Capital One, Comerica, Fluor, Morgan Stanley, and other organizations to find space for nearly nine hundred corporate moves. The Corporate Listings Department, which manages a large portfolio of foreclosed properties, sold 963 units last year. Ebby Builder Services recently landed sales and promotional responsibilities for a number of large-scale residential developments in the expanding areas of Carrollton, McKinney, Rockwall, and the Uptown section of Dallas. The Home Team Mortgage division produced $238 million in loans, and the Home Team Insurance Services division finished 2007 with a whopping 735 percent increase in revenue over 2006. These supporting divisions of Ebby Halliday Companies form a network of complementary services, management expertise, and experience that few other real estate firms can match.

In the company's most recent annual report, Mary Frances emphasized the company's focus on the future. "We realize we have to work smarter and harder to increase our market share and maintain profitability. To that end, we have experienced several years of capital expansion of facilities and infrastructure and are well positioned for growth." What exactly that growth will look like, the shape of the tools and technologies and services the company will offer in five, ten, or fifteen years is difficult to predict. What is predictable remains the spirit of the enterprise.

There is one thing about the company that Ebby would never change: its independence. "I have turned down many offers to sell," she said. "Companies want to buy us, to franchise us. I've elected to keep the company independent, and to ensure that happens, I've transferred stock to the people who helped build it. I have management in place to carry the company another fifty years."

Ebby's career was a process of self-discovery, an odyssey, and the stuff of legend. She sold tins of Cloverine Salve to Depression-era farmers, hats to wealthy socialites, little cement houses to first-time buyers, and tens of thousands of homes to Dallas-area home buyers. Along the way, she fell in love with FBI Special Agent Maurice Acers, a man she adored and "the best thing that ever happened to me," she said. "You want to know the secret of success?" Ebby asks audiences across the country. "Make people feel that you are interested in them. Make them feel special. Make it real. That's what Maurice did for me."

Portrait of Ebby (1963).

Ebby (right) age three with a friend who dragged her out of
a mud puddle to pose for a photograph.

View to the east on Elm Street in Downtown Dallas (1943). Ebby began her Dallas career at the W.A. Green Store in 1938.

Cloverine Salve is still sold today, although not by school children on horseback, as Ebby did from 1919 to 1925. In those days, the price was ten cents per can.

Ebby, age twenty, standing in front of a friend's 1929 Ford convertible, complete with rumble seat.

Maurice enjoys a horse ride during his tenure as Special Agent in
Charge of the San Antonio office of the FBI (1941).

Ebby poses with one of her hats that could be
worn five different ways (1940s).

Ebby pictured with her 1952 gold Cadillac, the first of its kind in Dallas.

Ebby with members of the Dallas Association of Realtors boarding a train for the statewide meeting of the Texas Association of Realtors in Austin (1952).

The second office of Ebby Halliday Realtors, located on Preston Road in Dallas, Texas (1953). Today, a multi-story bank building stands on the site.

Ebby watches as two of her young baseball players
demonstrate their techniques (1955).

Ebby (sixth from front) poses with the sales staff at the opening of the third office
(1955). She recruited female sales agents from the outset of her business career. Mary
Frances Burleson, then Ebby's secretary, is second from the right.

A Dallas department store window publicizes the October 1956 edition of *Charm Magazine* featuring Ebby and four other Dallas women.

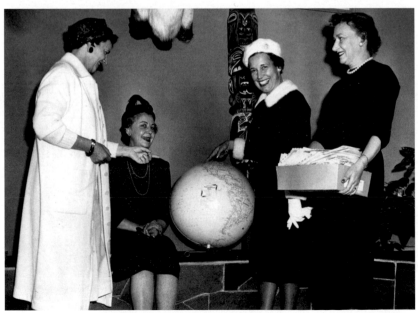

Ebby pointing to a globe when she visited the state of Alaska on her tours as president of the Women's Council of the National Association of Real Estate Brokers (1957).

Ebby (left) appears as a speaker to the Ohio Association of Real Estate Boards convention during her presidency of the Women's Council of the National Association of Real Estate Boards (1957).

Ebby photographed by Maurice in his Austin office shortly after they met in 1958.

Ebby in her Preston Center office, 1958.

Ebby and Realtor Guion Gregg (left) pose for a photograph of the first cooperative closing of an MLS sale in Dallas (1961). Roger Sullivan from Stewart Title looks on.

Ebby celebrates more than twenty-five years of sponsoring youth sports activities in the Dallas area (1961).

Ebby addresses Pennsylvania Realtors in 1962.

Ebby accepts the Woman of the Year Award from the Advertising and Sales Executives
Club of Kansas City (1962).

Ebby receives the Realtor of the Year Award from the
Texas Association of Realtors (1963).

Aerial photograph of the intersection of Preston Road and Northwest Highway shortly after Ebby's acquisition of the northwest corner lot and building in 1964.

The Derring Do Dozen. Ebby and Maurice's honeymoon in 1965 included her CPA, Bus Burgert and his wife Leonora; Ebby's secretary Mary Frances Burleson and her husband, Rufus; Maurice's CPA in Beaumont, Charles Neuman, and his wife, Fern; Maurice's secretary, Betty Turner, and her husband, Stan; and Maurice's CPA in Austin, Henry Ramsey and his wife, Betty. When asked in Mexico City by a reporter if she always traveled with an entourage, Ebby replied, "Only on big business deals and honeymoons."

Humble beginnings for Ebby's temporary Plano, Texas, office in the early 1960s.

Ebby (left), Paul Hanson, Mary Lou Muether, and Mary Frances Burleson
celebrate the opening of the Plano office in the mid-1960s.

Moving into spacious, modern quarters in Preston Center (1965).

The first corporate office of Ebby Halliday Realtors, located in Preston Center,
consisted of two converted duplexes joined by an atrium (1966).

Ebby and Maurice dancing the Texas Two-Step at a Texas-themed Rotary convention (1969). "Maurice was an excellent dancer," Ebby says.

Ebby in her office at the Little White House in 1966 with her brother,
Paul Hanson (left), and her husband, Maurice Acers.

Ebby surveys the Dallas skyline (1968).

Ebby presents Paul Harvey with a memento of his appearance as a guest speaker at the North Dallas Chamber of Commerce when Ebby served as president (1960s).

Ebby at FIABCI meeting in Copenhagen, Denmark (1967).

Ebby in her Preston Center office in the 1970s.

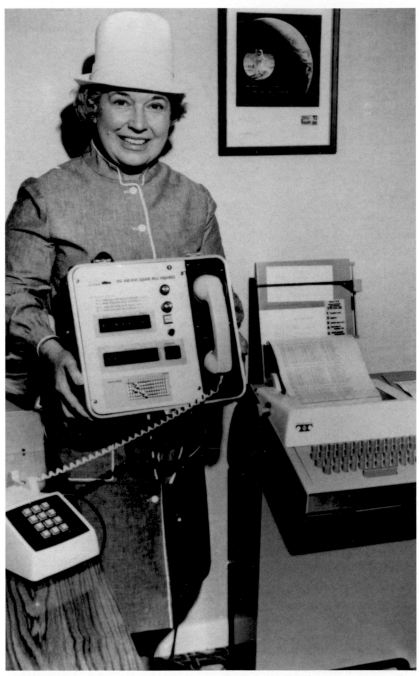

Ebby displays the latest technological advance—a computer modem and teletype machine linked to a computer in Detroit containing information about Dallas homes for sale. Ebby Halliday Realtors was an early adopter of the new technology (1970).

Texas Governor Dolph Briscoe, Ebby, Mrs. Briscoe and Maurice at a meeting of Keep Texas Beautiful. Maurice was president of the organization in 1973.

President Ronald Reagan welcomes Ebby to Washington, D.C., during NAR's legislative meetings.

Ebby in front of the "Little White House" office for a publicity shot.
She notes that the Rolls Royce was "borrowed for atmosphere."

The sports connection—George W. Bush, part owner of the Texas Rangers
baseball team; Tom Landry, former coach of the Dallas Cowboys;
Mrs. Tom Landry (Alicia); Ebby and Maurice (1990).

For many years, Ebby and Maurice celebrated his birthday
with a party at the Headliners Club in Austin (1980).

A photo montage of Ebby and her hats in celebration of fifty
years in the real estate business.

Fifty years after selling a development of insulated cement houses in
Dallas, Ebby walks the street where they still stand (1995).

Ebby and Maurice in their Dallas home (1992).

The executive management team: Ron Burgert, Mary Frances Burleson, Ebby, and Paul Hanson (2001).

Ebby celebrates a birthday at Dallas Baptist University (2004).

Ebby visits with President George W. Bush and First Lady
Laura Bush at the White House Christmas Dinner (2004).

Crowning her career of business and philanthropy, Ebby receives the highly prestigious
Horatio Alger Award in Washington, D.C., in 2005. Ebby is pictured here
with friend and nominator, Steve Durham.

Ebby welcoming visitors to the corporate boardroom
of Ebby Halliday Realtors (2007).

Ebby with the president of the National Association of Realtors, Dick Gaylord, at the hundredth anniversary celebration of the organization (2008). Ebby was named as honorary chair of the meeting, and she performed with her ukulele.

The National Association of Realtors hosted a surprise ninety-seventh birthday party for Ebby during the organization's one-hundredth anniversary celebration in May 2008 at its headquarters in Washington, D.C. The year also marked the sixty-third anniversary of Ebby Halliday Realtors. Shown here standing from left to right are: Kevin Sheehan, Betty Turner, Mary Frances Burleson, Rufus Burleson, Hanne Sagalowsky, Brooke Hunt, and Michael Hunt. Seated are: Lisa Sheehan and Ebby Halliday.

Today, Ebby Halliday Realtors and its related companies have thirty state-of-the art offices in the Dallas area. The contemporary In Town office on the perimeter of Downtown Dallas represents a commitment to the growing trend toward urban living.

Traditional, attractive branch offices, like the Allen, Texas, office pictured above, are well-located throughout Dallas and its suburbs. The company retains its longtime position as the largest independently owned residential real estate firm in Texas, and it currently ranks eleventh among the nation's largest residential brokers.